YIN YANG AND
PROSPER

How to Create a Thriving Feng Shui Practice

Lorrie Webb Grillo

YIN YANG AND PROSPER
How to Create a Thriving Feng Shui Practice
Copyright © 2020 by Lorrie Webb Grillo

ISBN: 978-1-7357287-0-4

Ebook ISBN: 978-1-7357287-1-1

Interior Formatting and Cover Art by: Rising Sign Books

Photo Credits: Pg. 74. Photo by Marcin Ciszewski on Unsplash.

Published by: Lorrie Webb Grillo, Thriving Spaces.

The journey of a thousand miles begins with a single step.

Lao Tzu

Acknowledgments

You will read about the assistance I have received as a feng shui consultant from my helpers—both seen and unseen—in Chapter 9, but this section is reserved for special thanks to those who helped bring this book into the world.

Wendell Fleming and **Louisa Jornayvaz** have inspired me and believed in me from the start of my journey as a feng shui consultant, and every day since. They were my first clients, first entrepreneurial gurus, first readers, and they continue to be my unabashed supporters and dear friends. Every note they so carefully and kindly wrote on my first draft was taken to heart and incorporated. Thank you, Wen and Lou, for your wisdom, friendship, and gentle pushes to keep going. I made it—thanks to both of you!

Terah Kathryn Collins is the founder of the Western School of Feng Shui, the best-selling author of many feng shui books, my teacher, mentor, and friend. Thank you, Terah, for reading and endorsing my book, for your supportive and helpful emails, and for your enthusiasm about this project. I am so grateful to have you in my life.

Nancy Silk is not only my editor, proofreader, and all-around cheerleader, she has been my best friend and sister-of-my-heart since 1975. I am very lucky to have a friend who is a professional copy editor, willing to read my manuscript countless times, and even come up with the title! *Yin Yang* (pronounced "yong") *and Prosper* is, well, perfect. I love it! Thank you, Na, for the many hours you spent making this book better. I'm singing your praises now and forever. (And if there is a mistake anywhere in the book, it's because I changed something AFTER you signed off on it.)

Kathleen Salidas, my book designer, has not only created a beautiful cover design that expresses my work, she has taught me about self-publishing and continues to give me confidence as I move forward. Thank you, Katie!

Jim Grillo, my husband and all-around foundation, supports my work, reminds me to rest, and is always ready to head out and play. Thanks, love.

Milo and Max Grillo, just for being you.

Contents

INTRODUCTION 1

What Is a Heart-Centered Business and Is This Book for Me?.......... 2

What Is Feng Shui? 3

I've Used the Bagua to Organize This Book...................... 6

CHAPTER 1 The Center: Your Stable Base 11

Start with a Sincere Mission................................. 12

Your Mission Leads to Setting Some Goals 12

What's in a Name? Everything. 12

Organize Your Business First 16

Meet My "Office" Suitemates 17

Learn a Simple Graphic Design Program That You'll Use................ 23

You've Got a Personal Assistant: Your Calendar Application.......... 24

Where is Your Business? Geolocation is Crucial 25

Get Paid!.. 25

Legitimize Your Business with the State and Set Up Your Office.... 27

CHAPTER 2 Career & Journey: How Do You Get to Where You Want to Go?.. 29

It Started in Childhood 29

What's Next on Your Journey? Think About Your Brand. 31

Your Website Is Essential to Your Business.................... 35

A Timeline Shows Your Path. Here's Mine. 37

CHAPTER 3 Knowledge & Self-Cultivation: Take Care of Yourself...... 46

Get to Know Your Habits 46

Things I Have Learned from My Favorite Books 51

A Note About Continuing Education 54

How to Stay on Top of Your Game 54

CHAPTER 4 Health & Family: You are the Chief Health Officer.......... 59

The Health of Your Business Is Decided by You 59

Set Your Goals, Then Price and Market Your Services to Reach Them.. 61

Choose Your Marketing Tools, Then Budget for Them 64

Some Thoughts on Second-Guessing Yourself and a Letter to the Reader 68

CHAPTER 5 Wealth & Prosperity: A Flow of Gratitude...................... 70

My Thoughts About Money. And, Yes, I Will Sound Crazy at First . 71

In a Heart-Centered Business, Do You Need a Contract? 75

Say Thank You for Your Abundance 80

CHAPTER 6 Fame & Reputation: The Golden Rule in Action.............. 83

How Does Integrity Show Up in Your Business? 83

Hold the Gasp. Be Nonjudgmental in Your Work.......................... 85

Own Who You Are and What You Do with Confidence 87

Use "Building Blocks" to Talk About Feng Shui 91

CHAPTER 7 Relationships: Get to Know Your Clients 95

Introduce Yourself and Invite Your Clients to Learn More. 95

Practice in Action: A Residential Feng Shui Consultation 99

Practice in Action: A Business Consultation 110

Practice in Action: Remote Consultations.................................... 115

Find Your Sweet Spot and Grow Your Business 117

Saying Good-Bye: To Hug or Not to Hug 122

CHAPTER 8 Creativity: Express Yourself and Connect with Others.. 123

The Family of Marketing Tools I Love and Use 124

Marketing Tools I Do NOT Use 132

Mistakes I've Made (So You Don't Have To) 134

CHAPTER 9 Helpful People & Travel: Meet My Helpers................. 138

My Helpers Are Legion! I Just Need to Ask. 138

Help is on the Way (an Example of Asking for Help).................... 143

The End is Also the Beginning 146

Chapter Notes.. 150

Introduction

This book tells my story of becoming a feng shui consultant, from reading my first article about feng shui to starting my business and confidently offering my professional services for the past eleven years.

I knew that I wanted to create a heart-centered business—one that cares as much about transforming the world as making a profit—and wondered what that might look like. Today, I know and love what that looks like, and I want to share the story of how I got here with you. I've written this book for anyone thinking about running a feng shui business and what it entails, from naming and marketing it to reaching your own definition of success. It's written for potential students of feng shui and budding practitioners, but the business lessons can be applied to any heart-centered business.

It was during a retreat, co-created and planned with two of my feng shui colleagues, that I realized how useful a guidebook could be for learning how to get this type of business off the ground and running smoothly. Our two-day retreat focused on mindset, marketing, and organization, and each of us spoke about those topics within the context of our own business. The attendees loved the information we shared with them and wanted more.

This is my attempt to fill that request for more. In these pages I open my office, my computer folders, my marketing and web-based applications. I share my favorite books, happiest moments, rookie mistakes, and what I actually *do* in my feng shui consultations. It's been a bumpy and joyful ride so far, and it would be a gigantic understatement to say that I've learned a lot on this journey! My hope is that this book will help you get started on your own journey and be a friendly voice when you are stalled or feeling a bit lost. By sharing the path I took to build my business I hope to illuminate yours, so you can spend less time stumbling and more time moving forward. I humbly share this story with you as a guide, not a textbook; one path, not the only path.

We often call a feng shui *business* a feng shui *practice*. (We call ourselves *practitioners*, after all!) This makes sense to me: in addition to learning the craft of feng shui to consult and gently teach our clients, we are taught to hold off on making claims, offering advice, and suggesting solutions without first understanding our clients and their goals. This takes practice! The concept of practice—as a business and an action—is the inspiration for the title of my book, *Yin Yang and Prosper: How to Create a Thriving Feng Shui Practice*. Practice requires listening and learning, which is yin energy, and then doing and mastering, which is yang energy. With each client appointment we are practicing, sharing our feng shui knowledge, and getting better at it. This book is about helping you to create a thriving practice for offering your services and prospering from doing it. By helping your clients arrange their environments to help them reach their goals, you create a ripple effect that shares your success and positive energy with others in a widening circle. By prospering in your own practice, you have the opportunity to help others succeed and thrive!

What Is a Heart-Centered Business and Is This Book for Me?

I first learned the term "heart-centered business" through my feng shui certification school, the Western School of Feng Shui (WSFS), and to me it means a business that is aligned with one's purpose and values. For me, that purpose is to be a helpful person in the world, bringing honesty and integrity to my work; to be aware of my own intuition about the spaces I enter; to bring my best self to all appointments; and to be clear about my fees and to work hard for them. It means I offer exceptional value for the services I provide in exchange for the money I earn. But money is only the byproduct of the work I love and am so grateful to be able to do. Money is wonderful, don't get me wrong, but it isn't the engine that runs my business.

What Is Feng Shui?

Because I use my feng shui consulting practice as the framework for this guidebook[1], it seems appropriate to define and explain it to those of you who aren't familiar with this ancient Chinese philosophy and how it is used to enhance our living spaces and our lives.

If you are a budding feng shui practitioner just finishing up your certification or diving deeper into your education, you may choose to bypass this section. Or you might like to know how I talk about feng shui with my clients, my workshop attendees, and my audiences, beginning with the correct pronunciation and a definition.

Did you know how to pronounce "feng shui" when you first saw it written? I did not! I said FENG SHOO-EE. That's certainly how it looks like it should sound. But I was wrong.

Let's start with the correct pronunciation: FUNG SHWAY.

What do these magical words mean? The simple definition I use is this: feng shui is the study and practice of arranging our environments to enhance our lives and help us reach our goals. It can be further defined as the practice of observing how our environment influences our health, wealth, and happi-

---

[1] As a Certified Practitioner of Essential Feng Shui® through the WSFS, I honor and follow the Eastern heritage of Form School Feng Shui while applying its practical uses for Western culture. Those of you familiar with other schools of feng shui will note the adherence to Form School rules and language. If you are not familiar with any schools of feng shui, don't worry, you'll learn something about feng shui along the way.

ness. It helps us solve issues in our lives by looking at how we express ourselves with the things we value. Feng shui makes a direct correlation between the quality of our lives and our environments.

That is a lot of meaning in just two little words, right? In English, they translate to "wind" and "water." How do we get so much definition from wind and water? Thousands of years of history, practice, trial and error, written documentation, and translation have brought feng shui to Western practitioners. It is believed that the concepts of feng shui originated with the spiritual masters living in the mountains and valleys of China thousands of years ago. These ancients studied nature and its forms—mountains, valleys, rivers—to help them understand how to live safely and harmoniously in the world. They saw that nature could be capricious and violent at the top of the mountain, where the wind howled, and at the bottom of the valley, where the river often flooded. Eventually they concluded that a spot halfway up the mountain was perfect—high enough to see invaders and be safe from flooding, yet low enough to be protected by the surrounding hills and mountains supporting them. This spot—balanced between the wind and the water—was thought to be ideal.

This is where we want to live today, balanced between the extremes. But we don't have to live halfway up a mountain (as lovely as that would be) to achieve balance. Feng shui can help us achieve metaphorical balance in our world and create an auspicious place to live, work, and play in harmony with everything around us.

What else is important to know about feng shui as you read this book? Here's a crash course:

Once the ancients looked at nature to help them understand *where* to live safely and comfortably in harmony with the world around them, they developed a system to explain *how* everything else in the world works. They saw that everything was imbued with a life force, called chi, that everything was connected, and that the world around them, and in them, was constantly changing. These are the guiding principles of feng shui that we follow today. From this foundation came the tools of our feng shui practice: yin and yang[2] balance, the Five Elements, and the Bagua.

Everything in the world, including us, is made up of chi, which is *alive, connected, and dynamic.* Understanding the nature of chi and how to use it is at the heart of feng shui. The ancients first understood chi as the relationship between equal counterbalanced forces: night and day, passive and active, female and male are just a few examples. They understood that these forces—which they called yin and yang—are two forms of energy so connected that one cannot exist without the other. As practitioners, we use yin and yang to help our clients find balance in their spaces between crowded and empty rooms, dark and light colors, smooth and textured surfaces. Yin and yang forces influence how we feel.

The ancients watched natural elements change over time: fire burning down to ash, ash turning to earth, and water nurturing plants. From these observations, they sorted all of nature into five elements: Fire, Earth, Metal, Water, and Wood. They believed that the interaction between these elements created everything, and that balancing them in our environment created harmony. Over time, the elements took on other qualities in the form of animate and inanimate energy, colors, shapes, seasons, directions, senses, and feelings, that are—you guessed it—alive, connected, and constantly changing. The world as we know it can be expressed as one or a mixture of the Five Elements, which, when balanced in a space changes the energy. As practitioners we recommend using the Five Elements—in their various

---

[2] Though it is common in the West to pronounce *yang* as if it rhymed with "sang," feng shui practitioners pronounce *yang* as if it were spelled "yong" and rhymes with "song." Try it and sound like a pro!

5

expressions—to make changes in our clients' work and living spaces to help them reach their goals.

The ancients viewed nature as a network of changing, interconnected events that eventually became a model for describing human transitions and stations. They divided these areas of life into eight categories which, in feng shui, are sometimes called "the treasures" and referred to as the Bagua, roughly translated as "eight areas." The Bagua is frequently drawn as a grid encompassing eight squares around a ninth in the center. It can be laid over the floor plan of a home, office, room, even a desk, to help locate those areas in a physical space. The eight grid boxes, each representing one of life's "treasures," are always drawn in equal size because they are considered to be of equal importance.

I use the Bagua grid with my clients to identify and locate the treasure areas in their homes and offices. Then I recommend changes using the tools described above to ignite and enhance opportunities for change in the corresponding areas of their lives.

I've Used the Bagua to Organize This Book

The Bagua is the perfect tool to help you organize your business for success. I thought it was the perfect tool to organize this book. You'll see a graphic of the Bagua grid at the start of each chapter to remind you of the equal importance of all aspects of your business and highlight where you are in the book. Each of the nine chapters covers one of the aspects—the treasures—of your business. You can flip to the chapter/Bagua area that you want to dig into or read the chapters sequentially. It all starts with your mission, which is at the center of your business. So, I recommend you start with Chapter 1, The Center: Your Stable Base.

Wealth & Prosperity A Flow of Gratitude	Fame & Reputation The Golden Rule in Action	Relationships Get to Know Your Clients
Health & Family You Are the Chief Health Officer	The Center Your Stable Base	Creativity Express Yourself and Connect with Others
Knowledge & Self-Cultivation Take Care of Yourself	Career & Journey How Do You Get to Where You Want to Go?	Helpful People & Travel Meet My Helpers

Figure 1 The feng shui Bagua areas with their Western names and my treatment of them in the chapters of this book.

Chapter 1. The Center: Your Stable Base. The Center of the Bagua grid is all about stability. This is the place where everything begins. From a stable center, you can transition and move in any direction. I've made this the first chapter in the book because the central question behind starting a new business is: What is your mission? In this chapter I'll share my mission, my goals (which have changed over time), how I came up with the name of my business, my feelings about the myth of the "solopreneur," and how I organize my business and my office.

Chapter 2. Career & Journey: How Do You Get to Where You Want to Go? As your journey begins, your new identity can be expressed in your brand and your logo. These are the words and images that create a short-hand way to tell people who you are and what you do. You'll use those to create your website, an essential tool for your business. I'll describe my journey to becoming a feng shui practitioner and consultant. It started in childhood, but I fast-forward—via a timeline—to the parts that are relevant to getting my business off the ground.

Chapter 3. Knowledge & Self-Cultivation: Take Care of Yourself. How do you stay on top of your game? I'll discuss important habits to cultivate, how to prepare for consultations, and give you a list of the business books that have taught and inspired me on this journey. I now attract my perfect customers and I learned how to do this from a book!

Chapter 4. Health & Family: You Are the Chief Health Officer. How's the health of your business and are you providing the services that people (actually) want? I'll go over some tools you can use to assess the health of your business and your menu of services. I'll discuss some of the ways I recover from rejection and the unhealthy habit of second-guessing my decisions.

Chapter 5. Wealth & Prosperity: A Flow of Gratitude. This is where you get to say, "Thank you for paying me for the service/s I LOVE to provide." Wealth and prosperity are about the flow of money into your business—not the accumulation. Money is an energy exchange and an expression of the value of your service. We all have money stories from our childhoods; I'll share mine and ask you to look at yours. Maybe you can create some new stories. I'll discuss gratitude and client contracts.

Chapter 6. Fame & Reputation: The Golden Rule in Action. Who are you? How would you like to be known in your business? Here's where you come up with your "rules of integrity" and your "elevator speech" so you can talk about your craft with confidence. I'll go over the importance of speaking engagements for getting your name out. I have been called "The Feng Shui Lady" many times, and I LOVE IT!

Chapter 7. Relationships: Get to Know Your Clients. You and your clients are in relationship! And as with any relationship, you want to learn more about the person you are in relationship with. How will you do this? I'll go over my client questionnaire, how I use it, and give you specifics about what I do in my consultations.

Chapter 8. Creativity: Express Yourself and Connect with Others. How can you use your creativity to market your business in ways that express who you are so you can attract your perfect clients/customers? In this chapter you'll find the marketing tools that work for me and the ones that don't (but which might work for you). Also, I've listed some of my trials and errors; I call them my top 10 fails.

Chapter 9. Helpful People & Travel: Meet My Helpers. Who are your helpers? This is an important question because we don't travel alone on this business journey, nor should we. I encourage you to find and invite helpers into your life. I'll introduce you to both my seen and unseen helpers, and how I find help when I need it.

Each chapter includes some exercises to help you move along the path of building your business. You may want to use a separate notebook to record your answers.

Now that you know how I've organized this book, come along to witness the birth and growth of my business, which started off kind of rocky because nobody liked the name I had in mind.

CHAPTER 1

Wealth & Prosperity	Fame & Reputation	Relationships
A Flow of Gratitude	The Golden Rule in Action	Get to Know Your Clients
Health & Family	**The Center**	**Creativity**
You Are the Chief Health Officer	Your Stable Base	Express Yourself and Connect with Others
Knowledge & Self-Cultivation	**Career & Journey**	**Helpful People & Travel**
Take Care of Yourself	How Do You Get to Where You Want to Go?	Meet My Helpers

The Center: Your Stable Base

Imagine we are having coffee and I ask you why you are starting your business. What would you tell me? Your answer would be your mission statement! (Well, maybe with a little editing.) Once you can articulate why you're doing what you're doing, you can begin to create some goals for your business. In this chapter, you will learn about my mission, some of my early goals, how my "entrepreneurial gurus" helped me name my business and articulate my services, and how I organize my computer and my office. All of these activities helped me build a stable base upon which to grow my business.

Start with a Sincere Mission

I wrote my mission in 2008 on a small piece of paper, in pencil, and still have it taped to the back of my office door.

To help my clients reach their goals by using the positive energy, practical philosophy, and powerful tools of feng shui with confidence, clarity, and optimism.

In order to fulfill this mission, I had to have some clients!

Your Mission Leads to Setting Some Goals

My first goals were small and humble. After my certification in December 2008, I just wanted to get out in the world and start offering consultations. So, my first business goal was **to be hired** in my new professional capacity. To be hired, I had to have a name, some business cards, and some systems in place (like how to get paid).

What's in a Name? Everything.

One of the most enjoyable parts of starting your entrepreneurial life is naming your business! And I encourage you to get help when you do—I certainly needed it. I thought I could come up with a name that would be universally accepted and loved. I was the solopreneur[3], setting off alone to create my feng shui consulting business.

The first time I heard the word "solopreneur," I thought it sounded so cool and described exactly what I was: a "solo entrepreneur." A one-woman band.

_____

[3] I first heard this word on a podcast interview with Cara Chace of Pinterest fame. Later I read it in Jon Acuff's book *Finish*. Cara loved this word and its concept; Jon dispelled the theory that we do it all alone. I'm in Jon's camp.

Except that I'm not a solopreneur. And, I would venture to say, neither are you. I couldn't have built my business without all the people who've helped me over the years: my friends, my colleagues, my graphic designer, my website designer, my son/webmaster, my husband/accountant/tax guy, my teachers, my clients, and my entrepreneurial gurus, who you'll meet in a minute. The list goes on.

It's the ego that feeds the idea of the solopreneur. It's the ego that feeds the idea that we can and should "go it alone." And if we don't, somehow we feel we are less than. When I remember that I need help, but even more important—when I remember to ask for help—my life gets so much easier, and my business reaps the benefits.

I started asking for help a month after I finished the first part of my certification program in June 2008. In July, I created a group I called my "entrepreneurial gurus," composed of my son, Milo (a budding graphic artist and web designer), and four friends who had all allowed me to feng shui their homes and/or offices as part of my certification program. I asked them to meet with me to discuss my new business idea and sent them a survey with some key questions about how I should run my new business. I reserved a room at the local library for our meeting to create a more businesslike atmosphere than I could achieve around my kitchen table. My survey asked:

What does feng shui mean to you?
Is feng shui for everyone?
What do you think a consultation looks like?
What should my website have on it/in it?
How much should I charge?
What do you think my name should be? What names do you like?
(Here I gave them a list of words that I liked for them to play around with.)
Who is my perfect customer?
How will they find me?
What should my gift to clients be?

Their insight was invaluable, and I took all their advice, which I've paraphrased here from my notes:

- People need to know that it's not expensive to do and that it doesn't take a lot of time.

- People need to know the benefits, i.e., "What's in it for me?"

- You'll need to have some information before the appointment so you can "hit the ground running" when you get there. (This comment led me to create the questionnaire on my website.)

- You'll need testimonials and a photo on your website; people will want to "meet" you there.

- Give your clients different approaches to implementing your feng shui recommendations: low or no-cost, medium, and high-budget options.

- Regardless of the cost, all recommendations should be listed by priority—what is most important for realizing/experiencing change first.

- You need to explain feng shui in language people can understand.

One of the biggest issues I wanted to discuss was my business name. I gave them a list of words I liked individually that I had put together to create two-word names. Secretly, though, I had already chosen the name I wanted and thought I could lead them right to it.

The name I chose didn't even make their top five!

So, what was this name that I thought was so zippy and fun, interesting, and feng shui-ey, professional, yet approachable? It was . . .

Restful Zestful!

"Of course, one could always add Feng Shui as the tagline," I said when the overall response from the group was . . . silence.

"It sounds like an herbal tea," said one.

"I'm not sure what it's supposed to mean," said another.

My son just smiled. I had proudly offered up this name to him earlier and he was very diplomatic in his response. As in, "That's very nice, Mom." I should have known at that point it wasn't going to cut it.

The group reminded me that my business purpose, my "Why," is a powerful statement that should come across in my business name.

After a vote, the winning name was, and continues to be, Thriving Spaces, which my entrepreneurial gurus convinced me expressed what I wanted to do with my work *without* making it sound too Zen and possibly too laid back or too Chinese and therefore limited to Asian design. (Feng shui works with ANY design style.) On the positive side, my name was:

- Open to all sorts of interpretations. My gurus reminded me that if I ever wanted to go into another type of interior design, I could use this name.

- Easy to pronounce.

- Open to a wide variety of graphic interpretations for my logo.

Most importantly, it said what I hoped for my clients' spaces—that they thrive with energy and balance.

Honestly, they didn't have to convince me. I had asked for their advice and I was going to take it. After being in marketing for many years before this, I had come to the very important realization that I wasn't always right. The focus group had spoken. Was I disappointed? Yes, a little.

I named my business Thriving Spaces and my blog Restful Zestful. I was off to a great start, courtesy of some valuable insights from my team.

Some of you may choose your own name as your business name, which works very well for service businesses like ours. That isn't the direction I decided to go because I wanted to have some separation between my business life and my personal life. I have always had an issue with tooting my own horn, even though I have a background in marketing and PR. By creating a little distance between me and my business, I am able to talk with clients about the benefits of feng shui and focus the attention on their spaces instead of myself. This little sidestep helps me to feel gracious and confident without pushing me too far out of my comfort zone.

Coco Chanel might think I'm an idiot.

Exercise: Mission. Goals. Name.

Write out your mission. Think about the actions your mission inspires: these are your goals. Then create a list of words you love when you think about your business and invite feedback on them. If you want to use your own name, think about a tagline that describes what you do.

Organize Your Business First

Getting yourself organized from the beginning is easier than going full-speed ahead and then figuring out your systems afterward. I speak from experience, as I just jumped in and built my systems as the need arose. If I could do it over again, I would have had some organizing systems in place first.

I'm going to assume you have a smart mobile phone. If you don't, I believe you need one. Your voicemail should be friendly, professional, and include your business name. Keep this amazing device clean, uncluttered, and beautiful (just like your office and your home). You deserve a protective case for it in one of your brand colors. The apps on your phone can request and receive payment; create, send, and receive videos; send and receive texts and calls; educate you with podcasts, books, and online workshops; help you get to your clients' spaces via GPS; and keep track of your steps! Clean out your voicemails, update your operating system, and sync it with your computer, your new best friend.

I believe your organizing system begins with your computer and how you have it set up. Your computer is your friend, your partner, your brain, your memory, your communication system, your graphic helper, your marketing guru, your filing system, and your photo album. And that just scratches the surface of what this amazing piece of equipment can do for you.

Treat it well and back it up.

I am a hybrid computer system user, someone who learned all of her business skills in a Microsoft Office environment on a PC and then moved to Apple's MacOS. Are you a purist? Learned one system and stuck with it? I envy you. Here's how I organized my business around my skill set, which will be different than yours, but you'll get the gist.

I work on a Mac and happily don't have many security issues. But I am a firm believer in insurance, and I back up my computer every 30 days and **always** before we travel together. Please, please do this. (Stop now and back up your computer. We can talk later!)

Meet My "Office" Suitemates: Microsoft Outlook, Word, Excel, and PowerPoint

I use Microsoft Office 365 for Mac. This is how I bridge my two worlds. Of course, there are programs that Apple offers that mirror similar Microsoft programs. I learned all of my business skills on Microsoft Office, so I'm happy that Microsoft adapted those programs for Mac users.

Within the Microsoft Office 365 suite I use Outlook, Word, Excel, and PowerPoint. Mac users can do the same things with Apple's Mail, Pages, Numbers, and Keynote. Choose the programs that work for you and get them installed on your computer. You will need an email program (MS Outlook or Apple Mail), a word processor (MS Word or Apple Pages), a spreadsheet program (MS Excel or Apple Numbers), and a presentation program (MS PowerPoint or Apple Keynote). You will also need a calendar (this is included in Outlook, but I use the Mac Calendar and will explain why later).

Outlook: Say hello to your clients. Then stay in touch with them!

I have a love/hate relationship with email, and you may too. There is so much junk out there (defined differently by each of us!) and *yet,* **an email is *(usually) my first conversation with a potential client.***

I believe you must have a dedicated email address for your business that includes both your name and your business name. Mine is lwgrillo@thrivingspaces.com. Because I wanted to separate my business email from personal email but be able to read both in the same place, I created two email accounts in Outlook that would come to one window. I also set up a Gmail address to use for retail exchanges and other miscellaneous uses. I check that account separately. You can color code emails coming from different addresses (I have a lovely teal color for the questionnaire emails that are sent from my website, so I click on those first when they arrive in my inbox).

Many people want to read their emails on the servers they set them up on; e.g., with a Gmail account, you sign in on your Google browser page and read your email on the Google servers. I like my email to automatically download to my computer into Outlook. That way I know I have emails in two places: on the servers (Microsoft Office 365, Apple iCloud, Google, or my business webhosting service SiteGround), and on my computer, saved in

Outlook. It is another kind of insurance for me (though may seem like double duty and a headache to you).

One of the miracles of email communications is that they can be sorted and saved in folders. I recommend that you set up your folders early. You'll be happy you did. My favorite email folders are the folders I create for confirmed clients. All queries, including those that don't result in a new client, go into a different folder called Submissions, which I keep by year. It is especially useful to be able to re-read an email communication from a client or query from years ago to help me remember things about their space when I follow up or reconnect with them. I save all incoming emails and my responses so I have a complete record of communication.

Be sure to create a signature for your email communications that includes your business name, website address, email address, phone number, and logo. My signature also contains a link to my email marketing program, Mailchimp, where people can join my mailing list.

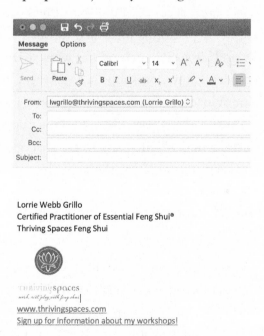

Figure 2 A screenshot of my email signature with logo and links to my website and sign-up sheet.

Word: Your word processing genius and helpmate!

For responding to queries on my website, I use email templates that I keep in a Word document on my Desktop and send via Outlook. For example, I have four different query responses—one each for residential, commercial, long-distance, and renter clients—which I can copy and paste into a response email along with a few sentences that uniquely address the issues raised by the person asking for information. This makes responding to emails efficient and fun. (See Chapter 1 notes for an example of how I use an email template.)

We all have content we need to write, and Microsoft Word makes it easy. When creating emails for a Mailchimp campaign (my web-based email marketing application you'll learn about later), I write everything in a Word doc first, and then cut and paste it into the Mailchimp template. When writing for my blog, I compose and edit my post in Word, and then cut and paste it into my WordPress account. (I use WordPress software to run my website. There are many platforms on which to build and run websites. Read the reviews and discuss your options with your website designer/builder.) When posting my workshops to local event calendars such as those on NextDoor or in local community newspapers, I write the descriptions in Word, and then cut and paste them into the calendar template set up by the event calendar hosts. Word plays nicely with various platforms so that I don't have to recreate and retype the same things over and over.

Excel: Keep track of your clients, income, and follow-up on one spreadsheet.

Excel is easy to use, read, and understand. I keep a separate Excel sheet for every year. I list my client's contact information in the left column, then use separate columns for the date, the type of service, how they pay (check, cash, PayPal/Venmo), thank you note date, follow-up email date, and how they connected with me: questionnaire, phone call, referral, email, or workshop. At the end of each month I use the addition function to calculate my total fees for the month and then check to make sure I've written all my thank you notes!

I don't keep track of my expenses on this spreadsheet, so I just see my gross income, which I look at once a month. I keep my expenses low, as I work from my home office and do most of my own marketing by creating materials in Canva, a web-based graphic design platform, and writing my own blogs and emails. I do have a few monthly expenses for applications I use like Microsoft Office 365, E-junkie, office supplies, some outside contract help with website upkeep, and administrative help. I pay most of my expenses directly using my company debit/credit card, which allows me to easily keep track of them online. I go over expenses and receipts with my tax accountant on a quarterly basis, and then tally them at the end of the year. (Some of you will want to keep a tighter rein on your expenses and I applaud you.)

PowerPoint: Your notes and prompter onstage!

PowerPoint is very easy to learn and has its own YouTube help videos (as do all of these programs and applications). If you don't already know this tool, I recommend using it to help you if you do any public speaking on behalf of your business. (See Chapter 6, Fame & Reputation, for my discussion on using speaking engagements to get your name out.)

I don't use PowerPoint for a short talk because committing to that kind of presentation means having to get to the venue early enough to either set up my own equipment or figure out theirs. For a short talk I'm usually part of another program, happy-hour information group, or networking event, and I need to be light on my feet and sometimes extemporaneous (e.g., not tied to a computer and projector).

For workshops or talks of an hour or more, I use slides (limiting the number to 30) for graphic interest, to illustrate a point, and to hold myself to my outline and time frame. If I caption them, I use as few words as possible. I don't like for my workshop attendees to have to read my slides. I don't often use videos in my presentations because they can take up too much time—time I'd rather use for Q&A at the end. While video can be a fun interlude in a PowerPoint slide presentation, you have to make sure it works beforehand. When it doesn't load or play (which I've seen happen many times at a workshop), the overall presentation is diminished.

I organize my PowerPoint presentations on my computer by topic, like Feng Shui for Health, for example. I include the subjects I go over in EVERY talk—the definition of feng shui, how it impacts our lives, some of the tools—along with corresponding slides I've created to illustrate those subjects. Then I customize each talk by creating new slides that speak directly to the audience at hand. With this method I can prepare a presentation that feels unique to each group but doesn't require me to re-create the wheel every time I give a talk on feng shui. I save each PowerPoint to my computer but also on a thumb drive so that if my computer bonks for any reason, I can plug into someone else's. (I usually ask the host of the workshop to have another computer on hand.) I used to hook up my own projector to my computer, but now I am more apt to connect a firewire from my computer to a TV (I carry a bag full of connectors), or send my presentation slides via a Dropbox email to the company or event center if they have their own system.

Figure 3 Using PowerPoint slides on a TV screen in a vision board workshop.

Learn a Simple Graphic Design Program That You'll Use

It is getting easier and easier to create simple graphic design for your business using online programs such as Canva, which I highly recommend. I also use Apple Pages to create notecards, notepads, flyers, workshop handouts, and Bagua grids for my clients' floor plans. Publisher is Microsoft's graphics software application that comes with Office 365.

Most of these programs allow you to import graphics, photos, and word processing documents to create an eye-catching presentation. It doesn't have to be fancy, but it should be clear and engaging for your audience. (See Chapter 1 notes for some of the pieces I've created in Canva.)

Of course, you can always hire a graphic artist for your graphic/marketing needs. It just takes a bit more time and money.

There are digital applications you can download to use on your phone or tablet for creating floor plans upon which you can lay the Bagua. Some of them have 2D and 3D options. There are lots of choices out there: SmartDraw, SketchUp, Planner5D are examples. I tried one of the earliest on the market, Magic Plan, because you can use the camera on your mobile device to build your floor plan, but I wasn't very good at it. I decided to create my floor plans in a program I am familiar with, Apple Pages, and insert online graphic floor plan elements, like furniture and doorways. My final design shows a general layout without exact dimensions, which has always worked well for my clients. (See a sample floor plan with a Bagua grid created in Apple Pages in Chapter 7, Figure 13.) Try out some apps (many have free options) and graphics programs and find one that works for you and your clients.

You've Got a Personal Assistant: Your Calendar Application

Being a hybrid computer user, I needed to figure out how to make the communication between my computer (MacBook Air), my phone (iPhone 8), and tablet (iPad) as seamless as possible. And by "seamless," I mean the communication never breaks down. This is the kind of thing a personal assistant does, right? Well, I've got one and you do, too. Your calendar application never forgets (if you tell it everything you want it to remember!). I use the calendar feature on my Mac to sync with my other Apple devices. For example, when I put a calendar date in my phone or on my computer or tablet, the other devices get it instantaneously. (Well, when they are in Wi-Fi connection with each other.) This is one of those digital miracles I am extremely grateful for. You can also sync your Google or Outlook calendar with your smart phone, but it takes a little more work. Sync your devices!

I use my calendar as a backup client management system, too. When I mark an appointment on my calendar, I type in my client's name, address, phone number, email address, and a link to the questionnaire I keep in their folder. This is all data that I also store in the Excel file I keep for my clients, separated by year. This way, I know that if one file becomes corrupted or I don't have all the data in one place, I can find the information I need in another place. And, of course, all that information is also contained in our email string, which is in each client's folder. Overkill? Perhaps, but I know myself well enough to admit that I don't always remember where I put stuff. So, having three places to stash it is good for me. Again, you decide how you want to store your information.

I use different color coding for business appointments, personal appointments, travel, and workouts. This is easy to set up in any calendar system and I recommend doing it for that quick look to see what your week entails. Plus, I set up reminder alerts one hour before I leave for my appointments to make sure I have enough time to prepare.

The best part about electronic calendars? Drum roll, please. You can scroll forward to mark a follow-up appointment or a check-in. When I return from an initial appointment with a client, I immediately schedule time to touch base with them in the future.

I also keep a wall calendar to get a big-picture look at my year. I put my workshops and speaking engagements on it as well as my planned travel, marking off the days and weeks I'll be out and about.

Where Is Your Business? Geolocation Is Crucial.

I use the street address of a shipping center where I keep a mailbox as my business address because I don't want my home listed as my business location. If you work from home, as many of us do, you can set up a P.O. Box that has an actual street address for use as your business address. Many print shops and UPS stores have post office boxes with street addresses you can use. This is a privacy issue for me, but equally important is having a street address to help with local internet searches for my services. My business address at the bottom of each of my website pages acts as a geolocator for Google searches. It gives my business a pin on the map, which aids with search engine optimization (SEO). The search terms that find me most often are *feng shui Denver*. These keywords help people find my business website.

Get Paid!

Rather than mixing business income with your personal finances, I think it makes sense to open a separate business account and credit/debit card. Select a bank that has mobile and online banking and works with services like Venmo. Being able to make mobile deposits is very handy and I highly recommend it. Setting up an account like this is easy and makes you feel like you're in business. Literally.

Now that you have a place to deposit the money you'll be making, you need to decide how you want to take payment. I accept checks, cash, and money transfers made through PayPal, Venmo, and E-junkie.

Checks and cash are great. I always carry a red envelope with me so that clients who pay with cash can place their payment in it and hand it back to me. We go over the power of the color red—Fire Element energy—that helps to initiate action and enhance implementation.

I sometimes use PayPal for long-distance clients or for those who want an invoice or receipt. I send my PayPal invoices directly from the application using a custom invoice that is easy to create from my account. As of this writing, PayPal charges a fee of 2.9% plus $.30 per transaction. If I invoice $150, my PayPal account receives $150 minus the service fee, which my client doesn't see. You can decide whether you want to add a service fee to your hourly rate for PayPal clients. I add $5/hour to any Skype/FaceTime appointment fee. PayPal accounts are set up to link directly to your bank account if you want to redirect funds there, but you can also spend them directly from your PayPal account.

Venmo is a handy peer-to-peer payment app on your phone that is securely linked to both your and your client's bank accounts, allowing for a quick exchange. You and your client must each have an account with a "handle" using the @ sign. The money moves directly from your client's bank account into yours. It's pretty seamless and can happen in the moment (at the end of an appointment, live or long-distance), or you can request payment later from the app. Currently there is no fee to use the app if the transaction is funded with a Venmo balance, a bank account, or debit card. Similar options may be available where you are, and some banks are creating their own apps, like Zell, to provide mobile payment services such as Venmo's. These applications may change their regulations and/or fees; check to make sure they work for you and your services.

E-junkie is a shopping cart service that costs $5 per month and allows you to receive payment for services or products through their website. Your clients can click on a link on your website, email marketing platform, Facebook, LinkedIn, or other social media sites to make their purchase. I create an E-junkie link when I sell admission to a paid workshop, like my vision board workshops which you'll learn about later. The payment links to my PayPal account and the money goes directly into that account.

Legitimize Your Business with the State and Set Up Your Office

I created a simple LLC (limited liability corporation) for my business with the Secretary of State's office in Colorado. It was very easy to sign up online. I pay a quarterly fee of $10 for the LLC designation, which makes me a legitimate business in Colorado. I file my business taxes with my personal tax return. Talk to a tax professional about the best way to set up your business and pay your taxes. There are options.

Now that you're aware of some organization tools, select ways to organize your business that seem easiest to you and won't take a lot of time to set up.

Take a peek into my office. (I wrote this section because I love to know what other people keep in their offices and thought you might, too.) Here's what's in mine—come on in!

- An L-shaped desk placed in the feng shui "command" position. When seated at my desk I face into the room, supported by a solid wall behind me. From this vantage point I can easily see the door. This puts me in a place of power and control over my space.
- Lamps! Overhead lights can be glaring, and lamps offer task lighting and decoration.
- Bookshelf. All my favorite titles inspire me.

- Art! I have a large painted canvas wall hanging of a queen with a dove in her crown. I am the queen of my office.

- My vision board. I have it hung in view of my desk so I can see it all the time. I stand in front of it every morning in the "power" position. (Thank you, Amy Cuddy[4]!)

- A whiteboard. I love to noodle around on this. When I want to change it, I take a photo of what's there, erase it, and move on. I got this idea from visiting a feng shui sister's office. (Thanks, Ro.)

- A large wall calendar for planning ahead, noting events, and trips.

- A small sofa for conversation, reading, and converting my office into a guest room.

- My educational and accreditation certificates.

- A large glass bowl filled with thank you cards from clients. I borrowed this idea as well. (If I'm feeling sluggish or down, I pick out a few to read. It's like pushing a reset button.)

Set up your office to help you be productive and creative, and express who you are.

Figure 4 My office. Come on in!

---

[4] In her book *Presence*, Amy Cuddy tells readers to stand in the "power" position—feet apart and arms overhead, like a 5-pointed star—to help them feel infused with confidence and power. Try it in an elevator before a meeting. It works!

CHAPTER 2

Wealth & Prosperity A Flow of Gratitude	Fame & Reputation The Golden Rule in Action	Relationships Get to Know Your Clients
Health & Family You Are the Chief Health Officer	The Center Your Stable Base	Creativity Express Yourself and Connect with Others
Knowledge & Self-Cultivation Take Care of Yourself	Career & Journey How Do You Get to Where You Want to Go?	Helpful People & Travel Meet My Helpers

Career & Journey:
How Do You Get to Where You Want to Go?

Assuming you've made it through Chapter 1 and have written up your mission, outlined a few goals, come up with a business name, and set up an organizational structure, you are ready to start moving from your stable center. Maybe you've even set up your office. Congratulations on beginning your journey. Before we talk shop, business cards, branding, and website, let me tell you a little about how I began mine.

It Started in Childhood

People often ask me how I got started as a feng shui consultant. It's usually not one of those careers little girls talk about when asked what they want to be when they grow up. Most of us in this profession have found our way here via circuitous paths through many different jobs along the way. Sound familiar? It's probably how you ended up in the career you're in today, too.

One of my colleagues was a scheduler in a dental office before she became a powerful feng shui teacher, practitioner, and business owner. I came by way of an Urban Planning degree, a stint as a city grant writer, then a position in marketing for a local real estate company. That's the path, but the seed was planted when I was a little girl and my father brought home a very special suitcase with a dollhouse inside.

Imagine a small square suitcase, like an old-fashioned trunk, resting open on its back hinges. The sides of the suitcase served as the exterior walls of the dollhouse. Looking into the case from above, I could see rooms delineated by vertical cardboard walls that popped up when the case was opened. The furniture was all jumbled up, but that created the fun as I could move it around however I wanted to. Dolls were also inside waiting for me to create stories for them as I moved them around their home.

It was so different from any dollhouse I had ever seen. I loved it. Traditional dollhouses are miniature houses that either have no front wall or you open the front like a French door and peer into it from the side. With this dollhouse I could peer into the rooms from above. It was a totally new perspective.

I played and played with my dollhouse-in-a-suitcase until I had to give it back. What I didn't know at the time (because I was a kid!) was that my father was in the midst of getting his PhD in speech and language therapy, and the dollhouse was a tool he used in the clinic to help diagnose and treat children by observing them play. It wasn't an actual *toy* dollhouse. It was a *therapeutic, diagnostic* tool. My dad wanted to test it out on me.

Today I realize that playing with that dollhouse was both therapeutic and diagnostic for me, too. In later years, trying to heal my own life by finding work that satisfied my soul, I discovered feng shui. In working with the Bagua, which looks at a space from above, I think back to that dollhouse and remember paying attention to how all the rooms were laid out. I like to think I was imagining the Bagua over them as I moved the dolls' furniture and accessories around to tell stories about them. This is what we do in feng shui—we move our stuff around to help us tell our stories. I was a budding feng shui practitioner!

I share this story at speaking engagements as a reminder that sometimes the work we love to do today can be traced back to our childhood selves.

I have never lost my love of dollhouses. That play turned into work I love to do—helping people understand and use the tools of feng shui to create the life they want to live.

What's Next on Your Journey? Think About Your Brand.

Most of us know what a logo is, but a brand is harder to pin down. I think of a brand as a shortcut to describe a service in a way that distinguishes it from other similar services. It is how people recognize you and know what you do. It should create a memorable impression and evoke feelings you want your clients to have after working with you. I think of brands in terms of words, colors, and images.

The words for my brand include "feng shui," "thriving," "energized," "practical," "doable," "fun," "joyful," "positive," "possible," and "support-ive." You'll find these words in my website copy.

Exercise: Start creating your brand.

Write some brand words, pick some colors, and think about images for your logo.

Start with a list of words that express your brand and that speak to who you are, what you'll be doing for your clients, and how you want them to feel after hiring you. You'll use these words in your website copy and in the promotional materials you disseminate.

Is there an image that pops into your head when you think about these words? Find some photos and graphic illustrations of those images for your brand. Notice the colors that make you smile. Keep your notes in a folder to give to your graphic and website designers.

Now that you have a name and a list of words for your brand, it's time for a logo, a graphic symbol that reflects your brand. Your logo can be used on your business cards, your website, and on any promotional materials you use in collaboration or affiliation with others.

A logo can be a typeface (e.g., Garamond) in a particular font (e.g., Bold Italic) alone, or a symbol, or both. If you use a typeface, make sure it is easily recognized by Google. This is the search engine most people will use when seeking your services, and you want to make it as easy as possible for them to find you. Some fancy typefaces and their fonts aren't easy to read by the bots that do the searching.

I encourage you to use a professional graphic designer to help you create the look you want. It will be with you for the life of your business and will work hard for you by bringing your brand to people through image. "A picture is a worth a thousand words" isn't just a pithy classic quote; it imparts a major truth about perception—an image can convey a story or feeling much faster than a verbal description can. Use your image to tell your story quickly, effectively, and beautifully.

My logo is a stylized lotus flower. In feng shui, the lotus symbolizes possibility and growth—two feelings I wanted my business to embrace and my clients to experience when working with my recommendations. Also, a lotus in full bloom is thriving and creates beauty in its space.

Figure 5 My logo.

Your designer may recommend colors, but I chose my logo and brand colors based on colors I love: teal, chocolate brown, and white. When I moved from working part time to full time, I wanted to be more visible. I felt newly energized about my work and decided that my lotus logo, in subdued dark brown, needed to reflect that energy. So, I had it blossom into a live photograph version in hot pink! While the colors of my brand and my logo didn't change, how I presented them on my business cards and website did.

Figure 6 From left to right, changes to my business cards from when I started in 2009 to today.

When working with a graphic designer, be specific about how many designs you want to choose from, and after you select one or two, how many color, typeface, and font iterations you want to see of them, and how many file formats you want the final version in. You will want several file options, including a vector file (this is usually an .eps file), a .jpg (or photo-type file), and one that can easily be inserted into a Word document (like a .pdf).

Ask your graphic designer to lay out your business cards so you can see how your logo and name work together in a small design format. This service should be included as part of the overall design fee.

If you're not ready to hire a graphic designer or want to try your hand at designing a logo yourself, I recommend using Canva. It has a number of great ideas for using typeface and symbols as logos. Canva also offers a fee-based registration with more options, but the free version is very robust.

OK—now you've got your name, words, and images for your brand, your logo, and your business cards! What's next? Your website! I've had two since I started.

Your Website Is Essential to Your Business

A website is a tool everyone should have today. It is your biography and résumé, your service menu, your informational brochure, your signage and advertising all rolled into one. It is out there working for you 24/7 without your lifting a finger, even while you sleep!

Websites can be passive or active. I believe that active is better; it keeps people engaged while they're learning about you. You can make websites active with a variety of tools—rotating photos, uploaded videos, regular blog posts, links to other areas of your site, and my personal favorite, a questionnaire, which you'll learn about in Chapter 7 on Relationships.

Start by searching the internet for websites you like (you probably already know which these are). Check out their navigation tabs and determine what you'll need for yours. Navigation tabs link visitors to sections of your website that contain more information about you and your business. Mine are: Home, FAQ, Services, Testimonials, Get Started, About Me, and Blog. Pretty self-explanatory. Remember your brand words? Use them in the copy you write for each section. I took a course through a local community college on how to write copy so online searchers interested in feng shui could find me. It was time and money well spent. One important tip I learned is to include your location (Denver, in my case) and what you do (feng shui consultant) on each of your navigation pages.

You can build your own website using an online template, but I chose to hire website designers who could design, write code, and build SEO (search engine optimization) into the code to create mine. I learned that Google Search works better with certain typefaces over others. As with choosing a typeface and font for your logo, make sure to select Google-friendly type-faces for your website, too. WordPress and Squarespace are two web-building platforms that most designers know how to work with. I use WordPress because it's known for being a bit more flexible, but Squarespace has templates and is considered easier to use. Having a website that I feel expresses my mission and how I share that with my clients is the best investment I've ever made in my business—and I've done it twice!

Why twice? Because I changed. After six years in business I felt like a different person than when I started—I had more confidence and I was moving from part-time feng shui consulting to my own definition of full time. I wanted to experience change in my business and my life, so I needed to change my environment, in this case, my website. I hired new web designers. The process of creating a website in 2015 was a little over HALF the price of the website I created in 2009. This was like a hug from the universe. First website: $3,000; new website: $1,800.

My new website is more vibrant, has a lighter background and new fonts, features a photo of me this time around and featured photos for my blog posts. I tightened the copy, changed out my services, and added rotating testimonials on the home page. It launched as I turned in my resignation from my marketing job to start my life as a "full-time" feng shui consultant. It felt like a rebirth. Here's a look at my journey from creating a part-time practice to a full-time business.

A Timeline Shows Your Path. Here's Mine.

Writing a timeline is a fun project to help you see where you've been and how far you've come. We don't often do this in life, even those of us who keep journals. A timeline is an edited, succinct version of events that forces you to look for patterns, "aha" moments, and shifts. It's always interesting what you remember about a past event while standing firmly in the present. Here's my timeline: fast-forwarding from dollhouse playing through several careers, I begin with the year I read my first article about feng shui.

Sometime in 2007. Read article about feng shui in the *Denver Post*. Have "aha" moment of realizing I've been "doing this" my whole life.

Ruminate while wondering how to bring feng shui into my life. Start reading books from the library.

Find my two favorites: *The Western Guide to Feng Shui* by Terah Kathryn Collins and *Move Your Stuff, Change Your Life* by Karen Rauch Carter. I read Terah's invitation at the end of her book to attend the Western School of Feng Shui and learn how to become a feng shui consultant. I felt like she was speaking to me.

June 2008. Tell family that I want to take my vacation alone this year. They are cool with this. Attend WSFS Practitioner Training in Carlsbad, CA. I'm going to feng shui school!

July 2008 – November 2008. Return home and begin my at-home-training follow-up. Am determined to finish by the end of the year.

December 2008. Turn in final written project, give oral presentation, and take test with two feng shui masters to complete my program. Become a Certified Practitioner of Essential Feng Shui® on December 2, 2008.

January 2009 – December 2009. Bring together my "entrepreneurial gurus." Ask for guidance on naming business and graphic images. Select my business name: Thriving Spaces. Add Feng Shui to the name in my marketing so people know exactly what I do.

Hire graphic designer to create logo. Use colors and fonts from logo to hire web designer to create my website. Launch website in June 2009!

Figure 7 A mock-up of my first website launched in June 2009.

Begin consultations on weekends and evenings. My first clients find me through the website and referrals from friends. Choose an email marketing program to begin building an email list. Send a quarterly newsletter, which ends up going out more sporadically than that.

Join Lowry Business Alliance in the community where I live.

January 2010. Offer first feng shui workshop at the Denver Public Library, Ross Cherry Creek branch, in January 2010. Some of my past clients attend.

Continue to offer feng shui consulting services part time in the evenings and weekends and expand services to include workshops.

Not much changes during the period 2010–2014 except for my desire to do more feng shui and less of my full-time work. Feng shui feeds my soul; my full-time job helps feed my family. Happily, they are not mutually exclusive, but my soul is crying out for more!

November 2014. The WSFS invites all alumni to its first WSFS Alumni Retreat in May 2015. I sign up in a heartbeat and volunteer to do a marketing survey.

February 2015. Research how feng shui practitioners market their businesses. It gets me thinking about my marketing and I consider creating a new website. The upcoming retreat and the research project are stirring the pot in a good way.

May 2015. Spend five glorious days at the retreat soaking up the connection, teaching, and love. Present my marketing survey findings. Thoroughly enjoy being with my feng shui sisters sharing insights and business ideas and learning new things. Decide to move ahead with the new website and hire designers.

Feel radically changed but don't quite know what it means.

June 2015. I know what it means: I want to quit my job.

Tell my boss I'm leaving and give him two months' notice. We decide to call it "retirement." I think it helps him to understand why I'm leaving, so I go along with it. But I also use a lot of other "re" words with my colleagues to explain why I'm leaving, like reinventing, reinvigorating, and reenergizing. In the meantime, my new website launches!

Figure 8 My new website launched in 2015; it continues to work well for me.

August 2015. Leave my position on August 31, 2015, and begin my life as a "full-time" feng shui practitioner. "Full-time" defined by me as: feng shui consulting and teaching as part of a full life of travel, writing, hanging with my adult kids, hiking, yoga, swimming, meditating, volunteering, reading, and being. ***My work now feels more like who I am as well as what I do. I feel some of the compartments in my brain disappear. I feel whole.***

September 2015. Nothing monumental happens, e.g., the phone doesn't ring off the hook nor do emails start pinging in. I dig into creating a new office space in one of our upstairs guest rooms.

October 2015. Take "Using Feng Shui Vision Board" workshop webinar through continuing education at WSFS. Start doing my own vision boards differently, using the feng shui organizing principles.

January 2016. Begin hosting vision board workshops using feng shui principles.

January 2016 – January 2018. Business picks up over time as I attract my perfect customers (you'll learn about this in Chapter 3) and engage with my vision board every day. I realize that with having control over my time, my wanderlust has kicked in. I want to travel more and now I can. I begin to set my goals around a calendar that allows for more travel.

Participate in WSFS private Facebook group of alumni practitioners and float idea of another retreat with other members. WSFS supports idea and two other feng shui consultant/sisters join me to create a weekend retreat set for June 2018 in Sedona, Arizona.

February 2018. Go on a bucket-list, life-changing active adventure in New Zealand. This trip is paid for with my feng shui consulting work.

January 2018 – May 2018. Work on agenda and logistics for weekend retreat with two feng shui colleagues. Love the process of working with them to blend our how-to-run-your-business program with some inspirational soul-sister community building.

June 2018. Host and participate in weekend retreat! Love the whole event: the teaching, the learning, and the connections. I am filled with gratitude for my work and this community. Want more!

August 2018. Listen to podcast called "Smart Passive Income" (Pat Flynn), and hear interview with Jon Acuff, author of *Finish*.

September 2018. Read Jon's book *Finish* and am totally inspired to write my own feng shui book about how I run my business. This idea has been bubbling since the retreat, when attendees asked for more information about our day-to-day activities such as how we market our services and attract and work with clients.

October 2018. Start writing. Follow Jon's rule on how to finish what you've started by selecting a finish date for my first draft.

November 2018. Almost forget to promote my vision board workshops scheduled for January! Set up three public workshops in various locations throughout city and send out feelers for private workshops.

December 2018. Set up three additional private vision board workshops. Create my own vision board and start planning trips for 2019.

January 2019. Start presenting workshops and get back to writing. Realize I need help with some of my administrative tasks. Talk to one of my feng shui sisters who has hired admin help. She reminds me of one of our feng shui techniques: to write the résumé of my "perfect" helper, place it in the silver box on my desk to activate it, and start talking about it. This silver box resides in the Helpful People & Travel area of my desk (lower right-hand corner). It's where I place all my requests to my unseen helpers (more on this in Chapter 9). The silver represents the Metal Element, which activates the energy of this Bagua area. I do everything recommended and find my perfect helper within 21 days! Note to self: Remember to use feng shui in your OWN business.

April 2019. Finish first draft of my book! Dance around office and tell family and friends. Decide to take a breather and prepare for two-week vacation. Am contacted by a publishing company asking would I be willing to write a book for them? Seems that all my writing and my daily affirmation asking the universe to send me opportunities has moved some energy in my world. This sounds too good to be true—and ultimately, it is. I find the timing and the contract too binding, and while very flattering, I decline. I thank them and let the opportunity go.

May 2019. Take my own advice: **work, REST, and PLAY.** Take a two-week walking trip in England. Am rejuvenated, rested, and inspired.

July 2019. Realize that my "breather" after finishing my first draft has morphed into eight weeks of no writing. Seek counsel from one of my entrepreneurial gurus who gently reminds me that I have "untethered myself from the project." She gooses me into action. Start working on (many) additional drafts.

August 2019 – October 2019. Drafts in process. Plan vision board workshops for January 2020.

December 2019. Move into smaller home as part of a plan to downsize.

January 2020. Host eight public and private vision board workshops. Am inspired by the visions of the attendees.

March 2020. The world stops for the Covid-19 pandemic and response. Am so grateful for my health and the health of my loved ones and community. Watch, wait, write, and pray for our world.

April 2020 to present. Reach out to clients, host live Zoom workshops, and do more remote consultations. Everything is changing. Connections to family, friends, and clients become lifelines.

Exercise: Write your timeline.

When I did this exercise for myself it was to remember the path I'd taken to get to my current place of peace and power with my business life. It was fun to do, and I recommend that you do this, too. Just like parents keep track of their children's milestones in baby books, writing a timeline is a bit like following "your baby" from its idea/inception stage to its launch and first steps.

After I wrote my timeline, I went back to look for patterns. It gave me the chance to be an anthropologist about my own life. It was a little uncomfortable, but interesting. Here are the patterns I see and the lessons I learned from them:

Pattern: I like to be invited to do things. It can be an actual invitation, like the one from author and teacher Terah Kathryn Collins at the end of her book to come to the WSFS and learn more. Or it can be that quiet, small voice in my head and heart urging me to find out more.

Lesson: On the one hand, this seems rather passive of me, but on the other, I would say that it doesn't really matter where an invitation comes from—a person, the voice in my head, or the universe. The point is to LISTEN for inspiration and then to ACT.

Pattern: Taking care of others before, and sometimes instead of, taking care of myself. I can see this pattern in some of the choices I made to not cause turbulence at work or at home. Turbulence isn't all bad; sometimes all you have to do is change course.

Lesson: Put your own oxygen mask on first!

Pattern: I had been looking for work/life balance for a very long time.

Lesson: Don't settle. With feng shui, I learned that I could achieve balance with work, rest, and play, and by creating a business that allowed me to truly express myself without giving everything else away—relationships, fun, and relaxation.

Pattern: I love to learn! Continuing education makes me so happy, feeds my soul, and expands how I think and act in the world: The Western School of Feng Shui, the WSFS Retreat in 2015, taking additional coursework about vision boards and space clearing, reading, podcasts.

Lesson: Taking classes, reading, and listening is fine—but putting it all to use is DIVINE!

Pattern: I believed I was supposed to be able to Do. It. All. Myself.

Lesson: Once you learn the power of asking for seen help (thank you again, entrepreneurial gurus) and getting it back in spades, you reach out for some truly powerful juju: your unseen helpers. Listening to these unseen helpers and acting upon their advice is one of my superpowers (and can be yours, too).

Pattern: I did a lot of wandering about in one career or another until I found my métier in feng shui. Did I waste my time?

Lesson: There is no wasted time! Don't bemoan the past and the wandering; it all has purpose. Own that and move forward. It will give you confidence.

CHAPTER 3

Wealth & Prosperity A Flow of Gratitude	**Fame & Reputation** The Golden Rule in Action	**Relationships** Get to Know Your Clients
Health & Family You Are the Chief Health Officer	**The Center** Your Stable Base	**Creativity** Express Yourself and Connect with Others
Knowledge & Self-Cultivation Take Care of Yourself	**Career & Journey** How Do You Get to Where You Want to Go?	**Helpful People & Travel** Meet My Helpers

Knowledge & Self-Cultivation: Take Care of Yourself

How do you stay on top of your game? Here are my good (and bad!) habits, a list of my favorite books, and a description of how I prepare for consultations, with time for rest and recovery.

Get to Know Your Habits

When it's just you, in your little office, with your cup of coffee, in your house on a Monday morning—what do you do? There is no one to talk to, there is no "weekly sales meeting" to attend and hear about everyone's goals for the week, there is no boss to check in with. There is only you. With your idea and a (hopefully) clean desk in front of you.

This is where good habits come into play, and it's important to have some. Whether it is setting up your office and file systems, creating a marketing plan, showing up on time for client appointments or networking events, your good habits tell you that you are going to give this business your best shot. Good habits will help you build a key ingredient in getting your business off the ground and out the door: Confidence.

If you are like me, you need help in the confidence department. Even the most confident people out there are writing books about how they don't have any confidence at all . . . until they get onstage or are in the studio belting out their mega-hit or putting paint on canvas. The gist of their stories is that we ALL have confidence issues that are specific to each of our precious psyches. Our confidence issues change over time. The questions we asked ourselves in high school such as, "Will anyone ask me to dance?" "Do I have BO?" and "Is that a pimple?" will transform into something different. Our new questions might be: "Did they like my report?" "Did I pick up the wrong fork?" "Will I make this sale?" And, hopefully not but maybe still: "Is that a pimple?" Our habits need to support our answers to these questions: Who do I want to be? What is my identity? Our habits have to change in step with our growing sense of confidence and shrinking list of things that hold us back.

Many books have been written about habits, bad ones we are trying to lose and good ones we are trying to build into a regular practice. Some bad ones might include checking email all the time, going on Facebook when your mind is wandering, and responding immediately to a text ding. Guilty! The first rule of breaking bad habits is to identify them. The above bad habits are easy to recognize and fix. But what if your bad habit is something that you're kind of proud of? My personal case in point is retreating into reading. I am a voracious reader. How could reading possibly be a bad habit, you ask? I'll tell you: When it takes up your entire day. When it gets in the way of having a conversation. When you want to hide in someone else's drama to put off delving into your own. Now that I've identified it, I catch myself and call myself out, gently and kindly, but still, I stop. Figure out your bad habits and then limit or cut them from your life. I have confidence in you.

Figuring out good business habits takes some trial-and-error time. You might try reading (OK, reading is *usually* good!) a handful of the plethora of business books out there. Some of my favorites, with their list of great habits, include: *The Success Principles*, by Jack Canfield (64 great habits), *The Answer*, by John Assaraf and Murray Smith (6 steps to reconditioning your neural pathways), and *Attracting Perfect Customers*, by Stacey Hall and Jan Brogniez (1 important habit: read your Strategic Attraction Plan every day to attract your perfect customers!). The point is, all these authors figured out what works for them, and you need to figure out what works for you.

I have four habits/actions I "do" every morning. They are not written in stone, but I did print and frame them in a lovely graphic I keep on my desk as a reminder.

I call them my Morning Rituals. They are:

1. Communicate with my vision board (stand in front of it in the power pose and look at each image)
2. Attract "my perfect customers" (by reviewing my Strategic Attraction Plan[5])
3. Check my email and junk folder
4. Check in with a client (it used to be "Post to my social media")

That's it! It takes me about fifteen minutes to get through my morning rituals and I feel so accomplished when I've completed them. I can get to work knowing I've reset my life vision (this is kind of like doing a forward

---

[5] The Strategic Attraction Plan is a four-page exercise in *Attracting Perfect Customers* that I revisit every year. See Chapter 3 notes for a copy of my plan for this year.

fold after a back bend in yoga to reset your spine), "called out" to the universe for my perfect customer and told them what I can do for them, quickly checked to see if any of my perfect customers and/or clients have checked in with me, reached out to anyone on my social media, or sent an email check-in or handwritten thank you note to a client.

Figure 9 One of my vision boards.

What I learned after my own trial and error of figuring out useful habits was that I need something short, sweet, and effective to move on with my day. I tried writing out a weekly schedule, which is fun for me as a planner, except that every week is different! But I've realized that I LOVE the fact that every week is different; that's why I work for myself.

The posting to social media part of Morning Ritual #4 was the hardest for me. It was on my list because I thought I should be doing it. But part of running my own business is identifying the "should dos" and deciding whether I really "should" do them or not. I've grown both wary and weary of social media in general, so I changed my fourth morning habit to a practice more in keeping with what I believe social media is all about: reaching out to people and connecting in a personal way on a subject that matters to me—feng shui. I can do this easier when crafting an email to a client than writing something I think a broad audience might appreciate on social media. I needed to change this habit so it would work for me.

I still use social media and I think you should too, but I only do so when I have some news to share (I'll be speaking to a group, hosting a new workshop, or posting a new blog). I usually have something to post about once every month. I do belong to a private Facebook group that both inspires me and needs me to participate, so I check in with them about once a week.

Many of you may have a meditation habit in the morning and I applaud you if you do. I usually meditate between 4:00 and 5:00 in the afternoon. I need this time to "dump the contents" of my brain before leaving work behind.

My morning rituals set me up to work. They make up my pre-flight routine every morning, so no matter what the day holds, I'm checked in and ready to go.

And if I don't do them? My business slows down.

Exercise: List your habits—good and bad!

List some of your bad habits as they relate to getting your business off the ground and running it—and think about ways you can change them.

List some of your good habits and rejoice! Look at them every day to remind yourself what a good businessperson you are. Then practice them every day!

(A great resource for identifying and changing your bad habits and creating and supporting good ones, is Atomic Habits by James Clear. I got this book for Christmas 2019. It didn't make this book's "list of top books" because I haven't read it several times through like the others you'll be introduced to below.)

Things I Have Learned from My Favorite Books

If you meet me for the first time at a cocktail party or other event, I will ask what you are reading or if you have a favorite book and share my own. I'll be so happy if this is a question you ask me! I will always have an answer (or two). One of them will almost always be in the how-to or business genres.

When I read business, creative, and how-to books, I actually (try to) DO what they recommend. I confess that I don't usually do the exercises the first time through, though. I just get too excited to get to the end of the book. So, then I have to read the book again. All of the books in the list below have been read more than once!

This happened to me with the book *Attracting Perfect Customers*, by Stacey Hall and Jan Brogniez, which I routinely recommended to the real estate agents I worked with in my full-time job. When I finally left that position to run my own feng shui business, I re-read the book and actually did the exercises—quickly realizing how powerful they were. And I started attracting perfect customers! I have a four-page Strategic Attraction Plan from the exercises in the book that I look at every day (this is the "Attract perfect customers" item in my morning rituals) and tweak and reconsider it every year. I highly recommend you do the exercises in *Attracting Perfect Customers* and create your own Strategic Attraction Plan. They work!

I think authors of business books must hope that at least one main idea sticks with their audience when they've finished reading. To put this theory to the test, I listed all my favorite entrepreneurial business books here and asked myself what the main idea was in each. I did this as a timed test, just to see if the main idea quickly popped into my head. If it didn't, the book didn't make the list. If you resonate with any of these main ideas, you might like to read the book!

Big Magic (Elizabeth Gilbert): Stay curious and don't worry about passion; curiosity will lead and inspire you.

The 4-hour Work Week (Tim Ferriss): You need to have a product that can sell while you are not working more than 4 hours per week.

The Big Leap (Gay Hendricks): You actually do have control over your time; it's called "Einstein Time."

Attracting Perfect Customers (Stacey Hall and Jan Brogniez): Imagine your perfect customers and welcome them into your life.

Essentialism (Greg McKeon): If the thing you are contemplating taking the time to do is not a Heck, Yes, it's an automatic Hell, No.

Finish (Jon Acuff): Starting is great, but finishing is better, and there are six tricks to getting there.

The Answer (John Assaraf and Murray Smith): You are in charge of your thoughts and create your reality.

These books are all meant to inspire and motivate and offer help along the way. But the only way they can help is if we remember what the authors are telling us. I focus on the "one main idea" because I am a terrible multitasker.

A person can't read only business books[6]. I engage my palate with all sorts of genres, and one of my favorites is how to stay healthy (mind, body, and spirit). Recently, while ruminating on why I wasn't busy (this happens in EVERY small business EVERYWHERE), I got nervous. When afflicted with anything, I turn to *Heal Your Body*, by Louise Hay. The one main idea in this book is: You can begin healing a physical or mental problem by using an affirmation to change your thinking. She lists afflictions and their affirmations alphabetically.

Under "Nervousness," the affirmation is:

I am on an endless journey through eternity and I have plenty of time. I communicate with my heart. All is well.

Let that flow through your mind, your heart, and your body and take a deep breath. I hope you're smiling because this sentence always puts a smile on my face and resonates deeply inside me.

It also reminds me that I have enough time to read all the books I want.

Exercise: Read!

If you are so inclined, read one of the above-mentioned books and see if you concur with what I chose as the "one main idea." I'd love to hear from you!

---

[6] See Chapter 3 notes for a list of my favorite feng shui books.

A Note About Continuing Education

Many industries have continuing education recommendations or require-ments for maintaining a professional certification. We feng shui practition-ers and heart-centered entrepreneurs must set our own standards for keeping ourselves up to date on new ways of doing business and learning new things that inspire us and inform our practices. (In 2020, for example, we all had to learn the ins and outs of Zoom.) You already know that reading is one of the ways I continue my education, but I also highly recommend that you join a networking or social media group, like a private Facebook page or monthly coaching call, sponsored by your school, a mentor, or other professional organizations. This is a place where you can post or speak to other practitioners on a regular basis, read their blogs, share your questions and your solutions to everyday and/or unique issues that come up in your practice (keeping personal client information confidential, of course). It's like being in a life-long classroom where you get to choose to ask a question, or not, and just soak it all up. It's a knowledge fest where I learn a thing or two every time I log or dial in. In addition, your certification school may also have continuing education programs and/or a blog or newsletter to keep you informed or offer a place for you to publish your insights. Find what works for you to keep yourself primed, keen, and diligent in your practice and do it!

How to Stay on Top of Your Game

When I first started doing consultations I would return to my car, drive home to my office, and almost collapse from exhaustion. Just from one, two-hour consultation! I wondered if this happened to other feng shui consultants or others in the counseling or helping fields. Were they also this drained of energy from giving so much in a consult?

I asked some colleagues and read about this phenomenon and tossed the *I Ching*[7] coins to see what the Sage had to say about this. I realized what was happening to me. I had been only partially preparing myself.

Here's what I was doing to **mentally** prepare for the consult:

- Reading up on what my clients wanted from the consult

- Doing some preparatory reading about their particular issue

- Google mapping their location and reviewing a satellite photo, if appropriate

- Checking out Realtor.com or other real estate websites to see photos or a floor plan of the home into which clients had just moved

- Printing my handouts

- Checking that I had all my tools in my briefcase

- Making sure my phone was charged

- Leaving a note for my husband with the client's name and address

- Making sure I had water and a snack in my car

- Leaving enough time to travel to the appointment location

- Claiming my no-judgment attitude

- Inviting my unseen helpers to join me and provide insight

---

[7] For those of you unfamiliar with the *I Ching*, it is a book of ancient wisdom that can be consulted for advice or insight into human nature and transitions. It uses the eight symbolic feng shui trigrams that make up the Bagua to create sixty-four hexagrams. You ask a question while holding three coins and "toss" them six times to create your hexagram, which has a number you can look up in the *I Ching* Hexagram Key. Open the book to that number/chapter in the *I Ching* to read the judgment and additional, often poetic, intuitive, profound advice. See my favorite *I Ching* book and guide in the chapter notes.

Here's what I was NOT doing: I was not ***emotionally and physically*** preparing for the consult!

Those of us coming to feng shui from other businesses or corporate work are very good at creating and implementing our to-do lists. We know how to plan and prepare for what we have coming up (an event, a consult, a presentation, a written report). We know how to get to work on time and stick to our schedules. We've sat at our desks and pumped it out. In fact, we brought this excellent work habit to our new practice of feng shui: our minds are fully equipped to do the work we have so carefully prepared for, studied, and been certified to do. We're ready to go and champing at the bit. All good stuff, right?

Except that feng shui asks us to bring our whole selves to the process, not just our minds. In massage therapy, therapists ask clients if they want a "full body massage." I realized that when I showed up for an appointment I wanted to offer something I'm calling a "full-body consultation": my mind, heart, spirit, and body arriving with my mind alert, all my senses primed to experience the space, an open heart to hear and feel my clients' needs and to help them achieve their goals with the resources they have. I needed to prepare my heart, spirit, and body, in addition to my mind, to maintain a healthy practice. I didn't want to just feel less exhausted at the end of a consultation; I wanted to feel exulted, excited, and energized. Not unlike the paradoxical feeling you get at the end of a great workout when you actually have more energy than you started with. I realized I could feel this way with preparation and practice. I needed to do all the things in my first (mental) list to prepare for each consult, but I also needed a regular daily practice (heart, spirit, and body) to keep me in business for the long haul.

Here's how I *now* maintain my optimal level of energy for my business:

- Expressing gratitude. If you're reading this, you either have or are contemplating heart-centered work. I know that you are thankful to be where you are right now. I am too. I wanted to make my gratitude an intentional practice. I do this by saying Thank You out loud for all the things I'm grateful for. Every day. It invariably brings a huge grin to my face. I often do this while driving. For me, it's better than listening to music! Some people have told me that keeping a gratitude journal is another way to bring presence and intentionality to their practice. Expressing gratitude opens my heart.

- Exercising six days per week. (Did I just lose you? Did you run out of the room screaming Nooooooo? Well, please keep reading to learn my definition of "exercise.") I mean move your body with joy. That's it. It could be dancing around the kitchen, skipping on the beach, taking a yoga class, swimming laps, hiking, biking, or taking a walk. Moving with joy is about acknowledging how amazing our bodies are and how wonderful it is that they take us to all the places we want to go, including to our clients' homes and businesses. Physical exercise certainly makes us stronger, and our practice calls for us to be strong (particularly if we move furniture). But it also quiets the mind and keeps the heart beating and healthy. Plus, it buoys the spirit.

- Practicing daily meditation. I've been doing this in fits and starts and occasional sustained periods, and I'm still not all that "good" at it. I've realized that even doing this badly is still better than NOT doing it. I wanted to quiet my busy mind, particularly at the end of the day. I use an app on my phone, "One Giant Mind," which acts like a buddy to keep me going. There are many meditation apps and classes out there; find one that works for you. I just sit down with my headphones for twenty minutes. This practice grounds me in the present and helps to put some breathing room between thought and speech.

- Learning new things. I love to learn new things that I can immediately put to use. There are many ways to exercise your imagination and do brain calisthenics. When consulting with clients I have to be able to come up with solutions to problems on the spot, and I believe this practice of learning new skills helps me to stay nimble. Find what is fun for you to do to stay inspired. Sudoku? Crossword puzzles? Knitting? Painting? Find it and do it!

- Communing with my vision board. This daily practice keeps me focused on the why of what I'm doing: creating a life that I love and that loves me back. It's all right there, pictorially represented on my board.

- Sleeping! In *Why We Sleep*, author Matthew Walker tells us that at minimum, we need eight hours of sleep per night. I'm at my peak with this quantity of sleep. And I do mean quantity. Quality is nice, but Walker's research suggests quantity is just as important. Sleep is something a lot of us take for granted, which I no longer do. I cherish this wonderful rejuvenation time. I now know that my brain is working while my body is resting to solidify what I need to remember and delete the other nonsense. If we promote the idea of balance to our clients, we need to practice it ourselves. Rest cannot be left to whatever remains of the day. It needs to be part of the plan. You probably already know the drill: little or no electronics an hour before bed; no caffeine after whatever time your body stops processing it (for me that's noon); a quiet, dark, and cool bedroom to retire in; a comfortable pillow and bed placed in the proper location in the room for a safe, secure, and totally relaxed place to spend the next eight hours; and a practice of going to bed and rising at the same time every day.

Then you get up and do it all again. What a privilege!

Exercise: How will you prepare to do your best work?

Make a list of the activities that will "prime your pump" to do the work you want to do. Post it where you can see it every day.

CHAPTER 4

Wealth & Prosperity A Flow of Gratitude	**Fame & Reputation** The Golden Rule in Action	**Relationships** Get to Know Your Clients
Health & Family You Are the Chief Health Officer	**The Center** Your Stable Base	**Creativity** Express Yourself and Connect with Others
Knowledge & Self-Cultivation Take Care of Yourself	**Career & Journey** How Do You Get to Where You Want to Go?	**Helpful People & Travel** Meet My Helpers

Health & Family: You Are the Chief Health Officer

You get to decide what a healthy business looks and feels like to you—how many hours you want to work, how many clients you want to serve, and what kinds of services you want to provide. In this chapter, I'll share the metrics I use to determine whether I'm on track to being "healthy" (by my own definition), the "family" of marketing tools I use to get to my healthy level, and what I do when I'm just not feelin' it.

The Health of Your Business Is Decided by You

What are the metrics (a fancy word for a variety of numbers you will generate with your business) you want to use to determine if your business is healthy? They might be the number of hours you want to work every day or per week, the number of clients you'd like to have per month, the number of workshop attendees you want in each workshop, the cost of your services, and the number of services you want to provide. A healthy business—by your own definition and standards—is a success.

You can ask yourself some questions to help you define success. My definition of success has changed over the years, and I imagine yours will too. Here are the questions I ask myself each year, along with my current answers:

What kind of business am I running? I am running a heart-centered, feng shui consulting practice in which I provide on-site and videoconferencing consultations, space-clearing and house blessings, on-site and online workshops, and in-person presentations about feng shui to interested audiences.

Who are my perfect customers? I never realized before I started this business that I get to decide who I want to work with! It is so freeing. You get to decide this, too. As I mentioned, I highly recommend reading *Attracting Perfect Customers* (Hall & Brogniez) and doing the exercises to help you manifest your perfect clients. I have prepared a four-page Strategic Attraction Plan from these exercises that I read each morning as part of my morning ritual. (See Chapter 3 notes for a copy of this plan.) It describes my perfect customers, what we have in common, what I will provide them as their perfect service, and how we are going to find each other! Here, briefly, are the customers I want to manifest:

*My perfect customers are **decisive** (they send a query or call and then make a decision), **open** (they are open to feng shui concepts), and **willing** (they are willing to take action and try my recommendations).*

What are my business goals? My business goals are to exceptionally serve my clients and gratefully receive payment which will support and enhance my life and allow me to give back. That's a good start, but I like to get specific, so I have some metrics to hit. I review and reset my goals every year.

(Remember that in the beginning my goal was just to have some clients!). Here are my latest business goals:

Finish my book and e-publish it on Amazon and my website. Edit my online vision board workshop and promote it. Continue to market the services I love to provide. Enjoy planned and yet-to-be-planned 2020 trips. Reach 100 attendees for my 2020 vision board workshops. Give with gratitude.

How am I going to reach my goals? I start by looking at my large 12-month wall calendar and scheduling important dates for workshops and trips (planned and dreamed of). Since this past year's goals included writing and editing, I put them in my weekly schedule in my computer calendar as a recurring "meeting" (with myself). You also know that I have a morning ritual, where I review my vision board and call to my perfect clients and read my affirmations. These actions—planning, reviewing and affirming—are all critical to reaching my goals.

To answer this question you can think about the services you are going to provide, how much you are going to charge for them, how often you will be working (full time or part time), the number of customers you will serve, and how you are going to reach those customers through your marketing. You can easily do this with a calculator.

Set Your Goals, Then Price and Market Your Services to Reach Them

You can go forward or backward with this analysis. For example, let's say you are starting your business on a part-time basis and work in the evenings and on Saturdays. You are hoping to have three clients per month for the first six months of the year and work up to five clients per month toward the end of the year. You can start with your services and price them to project how many clients you could have. For this example, let's say you charge $100/hour with a 2-hour minimum, so every consultation is $200.

Three consults/month ($200 x 3) = $600/month x 6 months = $3,600 for the first six months of the year.

Five feng shui consults/month ($200 x 5) in the second half of the year = $1,000/month x 6 months = $6.,000 for the second six months of the year.

$ 3,600 +
$ 6,000
$ 9,600 gross income

Congratulations! This would be an awesome year of gross income based on the research I did for the 2015 WSFS retreat that showed the average feng shui consultant made about $8,500/year.

You could also do this analysis starting with an annual financial goal of $9,600 and work "backward" to find out how many clients you would need to have, providing which services. To make this easy, let's say you want to provide consultations, divided evenly over the course of the year.

$9,600/$100 per hour = 96 hours. You have a minimum of a two-hour consult, so 96 hours/2 = 48 consultations. Forty-eight consultations divided by 12 months = 4 consults/month.

You now know how many consultations you'd like to do to reach your goal. When you provide other services, such as workshops or coaching, or products, such as e-books, you can add their sales into your financial goals.

I found over time that there were services I loved to provide, and others that I didn't. Today I offer the services that are a perfect fit for my skills, my goals, and my clients. Find what you do best and price your services according to the marketplace. One way to do this is to review similar types of businesses to get an idea of what the market will bear. Review, for example, what massage therapists, professional organizers, homeopathic healers, yoga, and Reiki instructors charge on an hourly basis.

Once you have your services list and prices, you're ready to invest in marketing. Marketing is simply the way you reach potential customers. It can be described as either a push or a pull action, and you need both to attract clients. You will either "pull" people into finding you with exciting content in a place that it is easy to find, e.g., your fabulous website, or "push" out your story (name, logo, and brand) and your services through your marketing activities, such as an email campaign.

Here's my "family" of marketing tools and what they do organized by pull, push, and hybrid marketing:

Pull marketing:

- **A website is pull.** People are online looking for services like yours. You want to "pull" them into your website through search engine optimization (SEO).
- **A blog is mostly pull.** I try to write a monthly blog on a feng shui subject that usually comes up during one of my consults. Or I promote my workshops. I use my blog as a link in social media posts.
- **Your business listing is pull.** Whatever organizations you belong to should have a business directory you can take advantage of as part of your membership. People searching will find you there.

Push marketing:

- **An email is push.** But don't be pushy or your readers will unsubscribe. Always provide value in an email.
- **A thank you note is push.** Yep, send one to EVERY client and anyone who helps you along the way.
- **A gift is push.** You give a gift either at the beginning or end of a service, or at the end of a workshop.

Hybrid marketing (push and pull):

- **A business card can be push and pull.** You give someone a card (push) and then they contact you later (pull).

- **Social media is both push and pull.** People find you and your profile gives you credibility.

- **Speaking/workshops are push, then pull.** You are giving information through this format (push) and people are receiving it (pull) and may contact you (yes!).

- **Video can be push and pull.** You can send video messages through your email marketing plan or you can post videos on social media that people find.

- **Online workshops are push and pull.** I market mine via Facebook and email marketing (push) and through workshops (push and pull).

Choose Your Marketing Tools, Then Budget for Them

(See Chapter 8 for more information on these tools and how I use them.)

This is where your expenses come in because implementing marketing means you'll be spending some money. In today's world, though, there is a LOT of marketing you can do without spending a lot of money and by spending your own time.

Here's what I spend my marketing budget on (some things are free!):

Website: It cost $1,800 to create and costs $50/month to maintain, both using outside contractors.

Professional photograph: $50 (I update at least every four years).

Business cards: The cost for 250 cards is $60.

Email marketing: I was using Constant Contact, which cost $20/month for under 500 contacts and included online chat and phone support. I learned a lot about email marketing using this program, but it was costly for me when I went over 500 contacts. I decided to switch to Mailchimp where I have a free plan which includes 2,000 contacts and lots of good online help articles, but it doesn't provide online chat and phone support.

Social media: Free! Don't miss out on this amazing marketing tool. You may already have a Facebook page. I use a Facebook for Business page and keep my personal page separate. LinkedIn is important if you are planning to provide feng shui services for businesses. I have a Pinterest account, too, where I have public folders on great feng shui articles and DIY projects that I can send via links to clients. I always post my workshops and a link to my monthly blog posts on my social media accounts.

Digital marketing tools: Many of these have free and subscription versions, or service fees: you get to decide which are worth paying for. I pay $5/month for E-junkie (this payment platform allows me to brand my workshops when selling them) and $14.99/month for Zoom (this upgraded service allows me to increase the length of the calls to over 40 minutes and gives me additional security and functionality for workshops and remote consults). PayPal charges a service fee for all invoices paid. I use the free versions of Canva, Dropbox, Google Analytics, Skype, Survey Monkey, Venmo, and What's App.

Blog: This is free in terms of money (no cost), but it takes time to write and post.

Gift: My gift is a small notepad (8 ½" x 5 ½" with 20 sheets). They cost $2/per x 250/year = $500. I give to each client and use as door prizes for workshops.

Business listing: I have several, but the most important one is the free Google listing. Sign up at once! The WSFS has a directory which you should use (I have gotten clients through this listing), and your certification program should also offer one. Keep your listings fresh and review them once per year. I also belong to the International Feng Shui Guild, which has a paid membership for consultants ($118/year at this time). They offer a directory and many free programs and services. If you choose to join a business group, it will cost to join. My membership in the Lowry Business Alliance costs $125 per year.

Branded thank you note: I designed mine on Canva. The cost for printing 200 is $250.

Video: My iPhone videos are free to create, but they take me hours to prepare, edit, and post.

Speaking/workshops: I am usually paid to speak, but there are always costs involved—thank you gifts, handout printing charges, gas or electricity for the car, time for setup, and Q & A afterward.

Sign-up form for workshops: The cost of colored paper and in-home printer ink. I create mine in Pages and print them four-up on an 8 ½" x 11" sheet. The form thanks people for coming to the workshop, asks for potential client's name and email address, and offers a list of potential services/workshops they can check if they're interested. One of my feng shui sisters swears by printing them on Goldenrod paper for attracting clients!

Online workshops: It cost me about $750 to create my first online workshop—$500 annual fee for the web-hosting platform and $250 for my videographer/editor. Then there was my time in creating the outline, script, and recording.

Of course, you will also have other business-related costs—computer, printer, paper and other office supplies, online or in-person workshops to keep up your training, meals out, travel, books. Just keep track of it. I office out of my home so I don't have rental costs associated with an outside office or shared space. Add these costs if you will office outside your home.

Now that you have an action plan, you can decide where you want to go with your business and what business success—and health—look like to you.

Exercise: Have fun and dream big.

Write down answers to the following:

> *What kind of business you have:*
>
> *At least one business goal, or several:*
>
> *A financial goal for a specific time period:*
>
> *A few traits of your perfect customer/s:*
>
> *One or two of your services and their prices:*
>
> *A few marketing tools for reaching your perfect customers with your services:*

Your answers should give you enough information to create a marketing plan and a course of action.

Some Thoughts on Second-Guessing Yourself and a Letter to the Reader

Dear newly minted, heart-centered business owner,

Have you second-guessed yourself today? Because if you're like me, you already have, or you will soon. I'm getting better at trusting myself, but I wanted to share some of my second-guessing habits so that you can identify your own and slay them.

More often than not, second-guessing keeps you static and not moving forward because you feel safer in the place you know. Sometimes safe can be more like stuck. For me, this can be creating four different email campaigns with the idea that one is sure to sing, but then deciding none of them is good enough and not sending an email at all. I wait for inspiration or for someone else to tell me which is the right one, or for the *I Ching* to give me the right hexagram that will give me the answer. (Ha! Readers of spiritual, philosophical, wisdom guides like the *I Ching* know they don't "tell" you what to do; it's up to you to decipher what the advice means.) We all have both seen and unseen helpers out there, but their job is to help, commiserate, listen, and suggest—not decide. Decisions are our job.

I have always admired Tony Robbins and followed him as an author, speaker, and life coach. What I've taken from his message is this: **The successful person has the ability to make a decision and act on it.**

When I first heard this, I thought, What? That is not a big deal. But then I realized that it is a big deal. In fact, it's the biggest deal of all. All of my life's biggest and best moments happened when I made a decision to do something. Tony is right. Making a decision and acting on it, even if it's off base, is better than staying stuck, in limbo, waiting for something to happen.

This is such an important business concept for you in this tender moment of starting and creating a life of work that feeds your soul. It's a time of tentative movement, a time of not being sure of yourself. I get it. I was there, and I frequently visit that place of not feeling confident. In fact, I don't want to scare you, but I've found that this feeling never completely goes away. It comes back to visit.

Making a decision and acting upon it is confidence building. It's one of those wonderful fake-it-till-you-make-it actions that allows you to put on the mantle of entrepreneur. And your action says: I am strong. I make decisions. I act upon them. I am a business owner.

Another form of second-guessing I have engaged in is getting stuck in research mode when I'm trying to solve a business problem. If reading one article about a topic is good, reading twenty must be better, right? This usually serves to confuse and upset me, but worse, stops me from making a decision. You will have your own ways to put decision-making on hold. Figure out what they are and stop doing them!

I now allow myself to read an article or listen to a podcast or read a blog about a subject I need help with. Then I usually ask a friend for advice and I always ask my unseen helpers for input during meditation. Then I sleep on it and decide. You will have your own allowances for research; those are mine and they've stopped me from wallowing around in research for weeks and gotten me into taking action instead.

Sometimes we just need someone to tell us that we can do it.

That's what I'm doing right now: telling you that you can do it. You can make decisions that will impact your business and you can move forward. Start now.

Love, Lorrie

CHAPTER 5

Wealth & Prosperity A Flow of Gratitude	**Fame & Reputation** The Golden Rule in Action	**Relationships** Get to Know Your Clients
Health & Family You Are the Chief Health Officer	**The Center** Your Stable Base	**Creativity** Express Yourself and Connect with Others
Knowledge & Self-Cultivation Take Care of Yourself	**Career & Journey** How Do You Get to Where You Want to Go?	**Helpful People & Travel** Meet My Helpers

Wealth & Prosperity: A Flow of Gratitude

Feng shui views money as an energy exchange, without judgment. Most of us, however, do have judgments, or feelings, about money and how it impacts us. Your feelings about money will impact your business and it's a good idea to know what they are. Why? Because, as a feng shui consultant, you will have clients who will want you to help them use feng shui to increase their wealth and prosperity. Practicing your own feng shui techniques to build prosperity in your business is a great place to start and give you confidence to share those same techniques with your clients. Of course, wealth and prosperity can be expressed and experienced in many ways other than through the exchange of money for goods and services. Whether it's money you're receiving for services or the glow from a gathering of friends, your wealth and prosperity begin with feelings of gratitude for what you have.

70

In this chapter, I'm going to discuss how important it is to know how you think about money and suggest some new ways of thinking about money. I will share my childhood money story and how I have created habits to change it. And I'll discuss client contracts and the two times since 2009 I haven't been paid my fee.

My Thoughts About Money. And, Yes, I Will Sound Crazy at First.

"Someday, when our ship comes in!" That's what my dad would say when my brothers and I wanted something that was deemed too expensive. Whatever the "it" was, it wasn't in the budget. But someday, maybe we could have it. Only as the years went by, our ship never came in and someday didn't arrive. Of course, this message wasn't meant to be buried deep in my subconscious to grow into an enormous and yawning belief about lack. Dad thought it was funny, a way to laugh our disappointment away and change the subject.

That faraway ship became the foundation of my beliefs about money: the ship isn't coming in; it's out there in the harbor and we can see it, but it's not going to dock. On it are all the things we could want, but we're probably not going to get them. Live with it.

I've thought a lot about that ship over the years and wondered what would happen if it were to dock. I decided that it might be better, since it probably was never going to "come in" anyway, to stop wanting it to come in at all. I looked for messages in cultural stories, books, and movies along the way to support the idea that money is bad for you! Such as:

- Money can change you and turn you into a bad person.

- If you like money, you might be someone who doesn't care about others.

- Having money means you could be cold and selfish.

71

- Having money means you are vulnerable. You could become someone that others will want to rob or hurt!

It made me feel like a better person to not want what was on that "ship."

Here's the part where you could be forgiven for thinking I've totally lost it. When my children were in elementary school, I purchased $5 lottery tickets for their Christmas stockings. Then, as Christmas morning arrived, and the lottery fund had grown into a huge sum, I became nervous that one of my kids might win! I am NOT kidding you. Later, when they got older, I told them about my earlier unfounded worries—because, surprise, they never won—and they thought I was insane. I don't disagree. I was lost in the fear of what might happen IF THEY WON BIG, e.g. the "ship" docked, and they would be kidnapped and held for ransom!

I wish I was making that up.

I fooled myself into thinking I had it figured out. My path from thought to action was this: It's best to stay below some invisible line of wealth so that no one notices you. Be modest. Be humble. Just get by with enough to cover your head with a home, cover your table with food, have a comfortable life, and hope no one will envy you. You probably won't get noticed, and that's just fine! For goodness sake, don't buy a yacht! As you can imagine, I was terrible about asking for a raise.

But what if having your own business, being in charge of your own time, defining what success means to you is your metaphorical "ship"? It was mine, and for it to come into the harbor and be prepared to sail, I was going to have to change my beliefs.

First, I forgave my dad. He was a child of the Depression and he was trying to help my brothers and me understand the world and not be disappointed by it. He believed there was a possibility (slim) of getting what we wanted, but that we shouldn't count on it. He was hopeful for us though: our ship was, after all, out there on the horizon.

I acknowledge that everybody has personal (read: weird) beliefs about money to sort through. Mine are associated with a ship.

Those beliefs result in feelings about money. Mine were associated with feelings of lack. Feelings run the show! You have to understand your beliefs to figure out why you feel the way you do. When I change my beliefs, it's easier to change how I feel, and then act.

Here are the actions I take to help me change my beliefs about money from lack to abundance:

I am grateful. Gratitude is the source of all prosperity. Whatever we're grateful for, we reap in spades. I say my "gratitudes" every day, usually in the car as I'm driving somewhere. I say thank you aloud for all the things I'm so very grateful for—from my happy childhood to having a good hair day. It's all in there, including having you as a reader of my book.

I imagine my "ship." It's a beauty. It's large enough for everyone I love to be on it with me. It has all the bells and whistles, including a private chef, massage therapist, and yoga instructor. The seas aren't always calm, but it's a very safe ship. I can come and go as I please and it's ALWAYS in the harbor, coming into dock when I need it.

Figure 10 You're welcome to come aboard! Photo by Marcin Ciszewski on Unsplash.

I read and speak aloud my affirmations. Every day. Yes, there's one in there about the aforementioned ship.

I take care of myself physically and mentally. Nothing makes me feel prosperous like having the luxury of time to take care of myself with a yoga class or twenty precious minutes of meditation.

I forgive myself when I lapse into my old beliefs, which I do far more frequently than I'd like, but less than I did before I started my practice of changing them.

I haven't bought a lottery ticket in years.

Exercises: Write your past and present money stories.

What are the stories you were told about money when you were a kid?

Have your thoughts about money changed over time?

What are your feelings about money?

Good/bad. Selfish/unselfish. Cold/warm. Complicated/simple. Easy/hard.

Write down some affirmations about money.

What are you grateful for? Make a list.

In a Heart-Centered Business, Do You Need a Contract?

Experiencing abundance means offering your valued service and receiving just compensation for it. To do this, do you need a contract with your clients? This is a personal preference based on what makes you confident and comfortable in a client relationship. Before going into the pros and cons of using a contract, I will assume that you have been in phone or email communication with the client before sending (or not sending) a contract. I've listed the pros first and then listed why I don't use a contract or a waiver form.

The pros of using a client contract:

It spells out exactly what you're going to do in the service provider/client relationship.

It can have as many disclaimers as makes sense to you, e.g., regarding moving furniture, making recommendations that are not guaranteed, not making suggestions regarding personal matters (a lot of personal matters come up in a feng shui consultation).

It outlines your fees by the hour and/or by square footage.

It can be sent prior to a consultation with questions you want your potential client to answer.

You can make space for just their signature or have space for your signature on it as well.

It is dated and contains all relevant client information, thus creating a data form if you need or want one.

It is professional and businesslike, creating the culture of the relationship.

Even as I write this list I'm thinking, Wow, this is a really good idea. Only I don't use one and here's why:

Contracts can be off-putting. They are used in cases where someone needs to be protected or where large sums of money are being exchanged. Who needs to be protected? This is a question you need to ask yourself about how you work with clients. Are you worried about payment? About them taking your recommendations the wrong way? About them blaming you if your feng shui recommendations don't work? About whether or not you'll break something? About whether you'll hurt yourself on the job when moving furniture or other items? These are all very important issues for you to consider. I've asked myself all of these questions. Dive into your own whys of needing or wanting a contract before you create one.

People "on the fence" about hiring a feng shui consultant in the first place may decide to hold off on hiring you when they hear they have to sign a contract beforehand.

Contracts are binding both ways—you are providing services; the client understands exactly what those are. Many service providers require signed waivers—massage therapists, for example—because they are touching your body. But many do not, such as hair stylists, who are touching your hair. A contract may bind you to perform but you may choose to not move forward, e.g., you get to the door and decide you don't want to work with the person who answers. If they've signed your contract, do you have to work with them? Probably not, if you included a provision in the contract giving you discretion to proceed or not proceed with services upon meeting the client. But who would? It implies that there is some test your clients must pass before you show up.

I think a written contract gets in the way of building this nascent client relationship.

So, what do I do? How do I capture client data, information about what the client needs and wants from a consultation, explain my services so they know what to expect and then procure payment? This has changed over the years, but I have a pretty sound system in place that works for me now.

Here is a recap of my client data-gathering and payment program:

Potential clients contact me via email, my website, phone call, or face-to-face meeting. I follow up with an email outlining my services, describing what we'll do in the consultation, reiterating that I consider their privacy paramount, asking them to set aside the time we need for the consultation, and presenting my fees. They follow up to schedule an appointment (or they don't) and give me any client information I need, such as their address, preferred phone number, and email address. If they haven't filled out the questionnaire on my website, I send them the link so I can learn more about what they are hoping to accomplish in the appointment. I send a confirmation email or text the day before an appointment to remind them I'm coming and to make sure I have the correct address. I query them about any parking or traffic issues that might come up.

Since I've been in business, I've had two clients who didn't pay me for my services. One was a retail business client who owned an upscale secondhand women's clothing store. She spent most of the appointment complaining about her landlord and her customers and commented throughout the appointment that she wouldn't do what I recommended. There is no judgment here; everyone has a right to complain about whatever they want, but this should have been a red flag that she probably would also be unhappy with me. If I'd had a contract with her, would she have paid me? I doubt it, as she went out of business shortly thereafter, which I found out when my letter requesting payment wasn't answered. I never heard from her again and learned a valuable lesson that changed my behavior: **I now ask for full payment at the end of the consult, even if my report is coming later.**

The other instance was a residential client who asked for a consultation and a report. She was unhappy with the report and didn't want to pay for it. This happened about four years into my working as a consultant, and I had never had anyone say anything but how thrilled they were with their consultations and reports. I count this as such a great learning experience for me because I had to own up to someone being unhappy with my services and someone pushing back. As a person who is conflict averse, I realized the universe was saying to me, "If you want to be in business, you have to deal with all sorts of situations, some of which may be unpleasant."

At the time, I needed to do some breathing and some thinking about how to handle the situation. I reviewed the first and second agreements in *The Four Agreements*[8] (Don Miguel Ruiz). They are: "Be Impeccable with your Word" and "Don't Take Anything Personally." I could do those things. Once I let go of taking the woman's unhappiness personally and reviewed the report I'd sent her to make sure it passed my excellence test, I was ready

---

[8] You will note that this book did NOT make my favorite book list (although it is a very good book) because I can never remember all four of the agreements. The first two stick with me, and that's probably because I am *still* working on them.

with a plan. I called and offered a negotiated price. She agreed immediately and paid me accordingly.

Here's what I remember about her from the appointment: she was a management consultant whose job was to negotiate contracts. During our consultation she told me she never paid full price for anything. Probably another hint as to what was coming. Also, I had billed her after I sent the report. I learned again, the hard way, to ask for payment at the end of an appointment. You might have noted that this is the SAME LESSON I needed to learn from the first situation. Unfortunately, it sometimes takes more than one "lesson" to teach me what I need to know. Has anyone else experienced this? Would a contract have solved this problem for me? Perhaps, although I doubt she would have signed one in the first place.

Though I don't use a written contract with clients, I do have written documentation, in the form of email communication, that describes what we are going to be doing together. It just doesn't look like a contract. It's written, but the only signatures are on the check at the end of the service (theirs) and on a thank you note (mine).

Is this policy set in stone? Do I always ask for payment at the end of a consultation? No, I don't. Sometimes I bill clients via PayPal or email invoice when they request it and/or use a bill-paying service. I then wait to be paid. I get to do this on occasion because I can; it's my business! You get to decide this, too.

Whether you opt to use a written contract or not, decide how you will inform your clients about your services, what they can expect during a consultation, what and how they will pay you, and what kind of follow-up they should expect.

Say Thank You for Your Abundance

I love to get paid for providing feng shui services and am very grateful that my clients find what I give them to be of value. It's a gratitude circle in which we each get what we want out of our transaction. At the end of the consultation we acknowledge the circle by passing the red envelope, which the client fills with their check or cash and hands back to me. At this point I express my gratitude for them. Usually they express it right back. The color red, which activates the energy of the Fire Element, encourages the client to put their new feng shui knowledge to use to help them reach their goals. This payment ceremony is a beautiful way to affirm our business connection and conclude our appointment.

When I'm working with clients who want more of something—money, love, customers—I tell them that having abundance is all about flow, not accumulation. When we think about acquiring or experiencing more of anything, we are usually thinking about accumulation! One of the easiest ways to achieve abundance in your business is to create opportunities for abundance to flow into and out of it. I call this sharing prosperity.

We can do many things to enhance the flow of abundance *into* our businesses. As feng shui practitioners we are in the happy position of knowing exactly where the Wealth & Prosperity areas are in our homes (including in all rooms), offices, and on our desks! We can boost these areas with the beautiful "wealth" colors of red, blue, and purple. We can open a window to bring in fresh air and help move out stale energy. We can hang a wind chime on the inside or outside corner of the space. We can be fastidious about keeping clutter away from this area. We can place images on our vision boards of what abundance looks like to us. We can start our day with gratitude. We can create great marketing and work our sales plans. We can write thank you notes to our clients. Abundance in, gratitude out.

What about creating abundant flow *out* of our businesses? Now I'm talking about abundance out, gratitude in. Providing excellent service to your clients is sending abundance out. When they pay and you use that abundance to purchase what you need to build your business, you create more abundance in the world. One idea for sharing prosperity is thanking your clients with a gift. I created a branded notepad that I give my clients at the beginning of their appointment to use, if they wish, to take notes.

Figure 11 My client gift—a branded Thriving Spaces notepad.

Another way to send abundance out to the world is to make a donation to a favorite nonprofit or contribute a gift certificate for your services as a bidding item for a fundraiser. Wrap up a gift certificate with one of your favorite feng shui books, a crystal, or a notepad, and you've got a beautiful "gift" to donate, and a write-off should you need one. Keeping up with continuing education is another way to use your abundance to build your business and create more abundance in the world. With so many options for learning, either remote or in person—Lynda.com, CreativeLive.com, podcasts, the WSFS or your certification school, community colleges, workshops, and retreats—there are many ways to feed your brain and soul. If you want your clients to follow your advice and counsel, it's always a good idea to follow it yourself. Feng shui doesn't operate in a vacuum and neither should you. Spending your abundance in the world—whether it's money or time or both—is a way for you to walk your talk.

Monetary payment is a form of abundance that can be received in a variety of ways today. Cash, checks, Venmo, and PayPal are the means I've described, but there's also Square and Apple Pay. You could also barter, doing a consultation in exchange for graphics work, web-master training, or social media content. It's truly up to you how you want to be paid for the value of your service. But make sure it's easy and convenient for you.

I have a friend and colleague who says that she is so happy doing her feng shui work that she doesn't even care if she gets paid! We have told her that she deserves to be paid and should be paid. In fact, behavioral economists would tell her that her clients need to pay her to legitimize the value of her advice. We all want our clients to take our advice because we know it's going to help them. We get where she's coming from, though, because sometimes it feels too good to be true to be paid for what we do.

Lucky us!

> ### Exercise: What are you grateful for?
>
> *Write a list of what you are grateful for TODAY. Think of how you would like to give back to your clients and community in ways that feel good to you and make sense for your business.*

CHAPTER 6

Wealth & Prosperity A Flow of Gratitude	Fame & Reputation The Golden Rule in Action	Relationships Get to Know Your Clients
Health & Family You Are the Chief Health Officer	The Center Your Stable Base	Creativity Express Yourself and Connect with Others
Knowledge & Self-Cultivation Take Care of Yourself	Career & Journey How Do You Get to Where You Want to Go?	Helpful People & Travel Meet My Helpers

Fame & Reputation: The Golden Rule in Action

This chapter is about aligning your values with how you do business. It's about treating others as you would like to be treated, and it's about telling your story with authority, honesty, and confidence. If you incorporate these values into your practice, you will be regarded as a person of integrity and earn an impeccable business reputation.

How Does Integrity Show Up in Your Business?

Feng shui tells us that all spaces are created equal. Equality is expressed in the feng shui tools of yin and yang and the Bagua. Yin and yang represent opposing but equal forces, and the Bagua is a model of life's experiences divided into eight categories of equal importance. This concept of equal treatment is a major facet of integrity.

Feng shui defines integrity to me: it's fair and equal; it honors all life, spaces, and things; it seeks balance; it's nonjudgmental. As a feng shui consultant, I hold and share these values as part of my practice. Principles of fairness, equality, connectedness, and change fuel my work, my practice, and my way of being with my clients.

I believe that being invited into someone's home is an honor and a privilege, and I treat it like I am entering sacred space. Home for any of us is where we get to be exactly who we are—the good, the bad, the ugly, the messy, the beautiful, and the cluttered. Our clients have invited us into this very special and private place to help them with some issue, problem, or question about how best to live in it. We are the diagnosticians and the healers. We show up with our tools—the Bagua, yin and yang balance, and the Five Elements—to help our clients reach their goals by acknowledging the many aspects of their lives and creating balance to enhance their spaces. The practice of feng shui is truly the work of balancing energy and expressing fairness and equality.

Our clients' stories are on display in their photos, books, furniture, accessories, colors, and artwork. Our job is to be attentive, to look, and to listen. Their life will be unfolding as we walk through and they discuss their home, pointing out their issues, their likes, and dislikes. The same is true of offices. Commercial spaces tell their own stories.

This is where your integrity shows up in the client relationship. Are you an honorable person in your work? Are you sincere and hopeful in bringing your ideas and recommendations into this budding relationship? Will you honor, without judgment, all the choices your client has made in their space? The "observe without judgment" caveat is of utmost importance. Your clients will be nervous about showing you their choices—as we all are when we enter into new relationships!

Hold the Gasp. Be Nonjudgmental in Your Work.

I'll give you an example of a difficult time I had withholding judgment when working with a client who, I would say now, was probably a "hoarder." It's one thing to say you come without judgment; it's quite another to walk into a client's space and be met with towering piles of furniture, boxes, artwork, food, books, and magazines that nearly reach the ceiling, and refrain from gasping with surprise. I was only able to do this—hold my gasp—because my client had warned me ahead of time that she had a problem with letting go of things. She had requested we talk a bit before entering her home. I felt that my work in that moment was to ensure that she was safe, that she could be comfortable, and that she felt seen and heard in our time together.

I realize how lucky I was to be tested about my own judgment in this way, and how grateful I am that she could teach me how to be better at my job as a helpful person.

It is in these moments with clients that we can compliment their wise choices, encourage their efforts to clean and/or straighten/declutter, ask questions to better understand choices they've made, and then recommend feng shui actions they can take. One of the highest compliments you can receive as a feng shui practitioner is to have your clients listen to your recommendations, implement them, and reap the benefits. The client in my example above called me again a year later to help her move into a new space.

While as a feng shui practitioner I don't take a Hippocratic oath, I do have my own set of "rules of integrity when working with clients":

- Show up on time. (Not early or late.)

- Meet the client where they are. In the above example I wasn't going to speak to my client about paint colors for her walls. I did make sure she had adequate room to prepare food and clear pathways to the exits.

85

- Make recommendations the client can realistically implement. It's not helpful or responsible to make recommendations that clients don't have the funds, time, or desire to implement. Additionally, I try not to recommend actions that don't make common sense, such as moving a garage because the client is worried it is located in their Wealth area or changing the location of a front door because it's not in an auspicious direction according to feng shui numerology. Besides, it is more creative to come up with cures for these kinds of issues.

- Coach gently. Feng shui can be learned and practiced, and I hope my clients take the knowledge I leave them with and continue using it to become their own feng shui practitioners.

- Do what I say I'll do. If that means sending paint sheet colors or emailing their digital report within a week, I do it. This is integrity in action.

- Hold the gasp! This is part of nonjudgment. I'm not saying I can't have an opinion to share when asked. I thoroughly applauded the client who wanted to turn her formal dining room into a mini roller-skating rink for herself and her kids.

Rules of integrity don't just apply when someone is watching, as in a client appointment. They are alive and well right in your office—when you set your prices, when you send your emails, when you offer services. Here are the rules I hold myself to in my business:

- Set prices equally. You may choose to set different prices for services rendered to nonprofit organizations, schools, and libraries versus for-profit commercial enterprises, but I don't recommend changing your prices based on the zip code of the homes or businesses you are serving. This would not only be hard to keep track of but would also not be treating everyone equally.

- Practice email etiquette. Think about how you collect email addresses. When I started, I was eager to build my email universe. When I was sent an email or a query through my website I "grabbed" the email address and added it to my mailing list. Since that time, after reading about email etiquette and receiving emails from places that have grabbed my address without my realizing it, I have changed my practice. People must opt in to receive email correspondence from me by checking a box. There's a huge plus in doing this: I have found that my "unsubscribes" from marketing emails have dropped off, and I feel better knowing that I'm sending information to people who want it.

- Keep to a regular schedule. I quit at 5 p.m. to go hang out with my family. If I'm asking my clients to live by my words—work, rest, play with feng shui—then I must attempt to live by them, too.

- Give credit where credit is due. I am very indebted to my many teachers and credit their ideas throughout my talks, consults, and in these pages. You'll see their names and their books and ideas throughout this book! Giving credit where it's due is a way to share good words and deeds.

- Practice some feng shui every day. Whether it's cleaning off my desk at the end of the day, constantly editing and culling my own closet and pantry, or treating myself to some beauty, exercise, and rest, I try to remember why I do what I do. This is a way to stay grounded in my own enterprise. I can—and should—be a helpful person to myself.

Speaking of which . . . it's nearly 5 p.m. See you later.

Own Who You Are and What You Do With Confidence

I recently spoke with a colleague from my "other life," the life before I became a feng shui consultant. She asked me how my *retirement* was going. I took a breath and remembered that this is what I told everyone when I left my job as a marketing VP. I said I was retiring but couched it with other "re-" words like reimagining and reinventing. What I didn't tell anyone was that I was going to plunge myself into developing my feng shui consulting business. I wasn't willing to say it at the time.

Why? Why didn't I proclaim that I was leaving my job to create my own dream work/life balance?

87

Here's why:

- Because I was afraid of failure.

- Because I didn't want people "watching" me to see how it was going. (And judging me, too.)

- Because I thought it would make them, all those people in the company I was leaving, ostensibly "feel better" that I wasn't leaving them, I simply was ready to leave working altogether! This was lame, and untrue.

- Because I wanted to see how it was all going to work in the quiet of my own office, with me working at something I truly love to do and hoping I could build it up, one client at a time, without too much fanfare. Under the radar, as it were. (This is another way of saying "fear of failure.")

Like me, many people were brought up to believe that we are here to help and support others, ensuring it all runs smoothly without needing to be acknowledged or thanked. I was too self-deprecating, hardly able to take a compliment, always giving credit to the "team" instead of accepting acknowledgment for my part. I would typically shrug off an accomplishment and accompanying accolade with a "yeah, thanks, but really, it was nothing." When I made nothing of it, the job, the accomplishment, became nothing too. I didn't understand this at the time. I do now.

The irony is that for many years, my work in marketing helped others sell their products or services. I excelled at this, so it should have been easy to transfer my marketing skills to my own business, right? Well, yes and no. Yes, I certainly have the tools: I love to write and design and know my limitations with those skills and hire out when I need to, and I am a reader of marketing blogs and books and I know how to apply what I learn to my own business. And yet, one of the best ways to market one's business is to network. This is where the "no" comes in. I don't love attending networking meetings and events and am not a joiner in general. My default RSVP is almost always a no.

As a self-diagnosed introvert and situational extrovert, I have to prepare myself when I do go to events. Of course, I usually enjoy myself, meeting people who are interested in what I do. But it's not my happy place.

My happy place is with my clients one-on-one in their space, sharing interesting ways to create an environment that will help them achieve their goals. I love to listen to what it is they want and to help them find ways that match their abilities to make their dreams come true. And here's the thing: I am good at this.

Look at what I just told you! I am making progress in my ability to own up to my own achievement.

This is what I want you to learn from my experience: find a level of confidence, not aggressive self-promotion, that allows you to talk about what you do without an "aw, shucks" shrug. Own up to your accomplishments—finishing your training, becoming certified and approved, starting your business—doing what you do *in the service of others*. You worked hard to get to this place of competence and excellence, and you can now speak about it with clarity and confidence and joy. How? Some people create what's called the "elevator speech." (Although I've been in many elevators in my life and have never heard one.) Elevator speeches are short and effective (hence the term), a short ride that gets you to where you want to go. But they always sound canned and practiced to me, so I don't have just one. I think it's fun to have a lot of different ways to talk about what you do depending on the circumstances. Here are a few that I use. Help yourself!

I help people change out the energy of their spaces.

I help people on the cusp of change make adjustments to their spaces to help them with the transition.

I review floor plans of remodels or new construction to help people make positive changes on paper before they get to the build-out phase.

I create and present blessing ceremonies for people selling their homes so they can say good-bye to them with gratitude and love.

I create ceremonies for people moving into a new space so they can express their hopes and dreams and invite the space to support them.

I help people balance the energy in their homes for peace and harmony.

That's a lot of "I" statements for a recovering, self-deprecating team player. And it's taken me a while to get to a place of peace in saying them. What I have found is that people respond to these statements with interest, understanding, and often a smile or a question.

Here's what I wish I had said to all those folks in my "other life" when I left my job:

I'm leaving this job to do work that is calling to me at this time. I'm going to build my feng shui business in a way that works with the overall goals of my life as they unfold and as my life changes. I am reinventing work for myself and I am off on an adventure.

I told that former colleague on the phone that I hadn't actually retired, that I was happily offering feng shui services through my company and having the time of my life. She was very happy for me!

Exercise: Tell people what you do.

How do you answer when people ask about the work you do? Write a response (or more than one) that you could give at a picnic, a cocktail party, or even in an elevator! Then practice it with friends or in front of the mirror.

Use "Building Blocks" to Talk About Feng Shui

I love to talk about feng shui when asked. It's my study, my practice, my work, and literally my viewpoint; I can't *not* see through "feng shui" eyes. But because it is such a part of me, I often have a hard time remembering how I started to learn about it. Sometimes it feels like I've always known.

This is an issue for me when I talk about feng shui in conversation or when speaking to groups. I need to remember that my listeners haven't spent years reading, thinking, or consulting about it. You may experience this with your own specialty when asked about it.

When I began to speak publicly about feng shui, I wanted to create building blocks so that people could learn as much as made sense to them and continue if they wanted more. I started to think about it like math. You need arithmetic as a life skill, to balance your checkbook and manage your money. You need geometry and calculus if you want to build a bridge. I wanted to come up with a way to talk about feng shui in a way that people who only wanted to know the "arithmetic" version could get started and make some positive changes in their lives, as well as spark the interest of those who wanted a "higher math" version.

Here are the building blocks I use in my talks and workshops to introduce the concepts of feng shui:

1. I always start with an easy-to-understand definition: *Feng shui is the study and practice of arranging our environments to enhance our lives and help us reach our goals.*

2. What should you address first? I always start with safety, and from there move to comfort and beauty. People are often surprised when I begin by discussing safety, but they connect with how important it is to feel safe in your space before decorating it. No one wants to walk up a dark path to get to a front door, trip on a broken step, or get their key stuck in a lock. If people fix their "broken" things and makes their spaces safe first, they are practicing excellent feng shui!

3. Balance your work, rest, and play in life and in your spaces. This is a great place to bring up the Goldilocks story. All of us are looking for a life that is "not too hot or too cold, too little or too big, too hard or too soft." We want things to be "just right." (My teacher and mentor, Terah Kathryn Collins of the WSFS, told this story on the first day of our feng shui certification training and it resonated with me. I knew it would also resonate with others. Thanks, Terah!) We are better, happier humans when we acknowledge the need for balance in our lives and that our spaces can support this need.

4. There is no hierarchy of spaces in your home or office. I talk about room usage (places to eat and sleep, places to rest and play, places to work and create) and the democracy of spaces. The living room is not more important than the pantry!

This is a great place to stop if I only have a short time to talk or have been asked to give a quick, twenty-minute overview. With more time I offer the following:

5. Feng shui originated in ancient China over 3,000 years ago; it's a cultural design practice translated for today. It's not just for Asian design aficionados; feng shui works with all design styles.

6. The three tenets of feng shui mirror the principles of quantum physics: all things are alive, connected, and changing.

7. Everyone knows something about yin and yang as an expression of female and male. I give them other examples of yin and yang and explain that they are important facets of feng shui because they represent duality in our world and the constancy of change.

8. The vital life force, called chi, infuses all things. It animates yin and yang and is further expressed in the Five Elements: Fire, Earth, Metal, Water, and Wood.

9. We are in relationship not only with our family and friends, but with our things and our spaces. When we put time and energy into our human relationships, they flourish! The same can be said of our relationship with our spaces.

When I have up to two hours to talk and am able to use PowerPoint slides to visually punctuate the ideas, I move to the "higher math" version:

10. Our lives can be mapped out on a grid laid over our spaces—homes, offices, rooms, desk. This grid is called the Bagua, the feng shui model of life's experiences divided into eight categories. It is often drawn as a grid with eight equal-sized boxes around a ninth, central box of the same size. These areas represent stations of human life, sometimes referred to as life's "treasures."

11. How do you use the Bagua? Draw the grid lines over a floor plan, encompassing all areas under the roof line, including any attached rooms such as garages. Ensure that all nine boxes are the same size.

12. Use the Five Elements—Fire, Earth, Metal, Water, and Wood—and their expressions through color, shape, and material to enhance those areas in the Bagua you want to draw energy to.

13. What are some great enhancements we all can make? Here I cover the best placement for beds and desks, where to hang art on your walls, and how to create a welcoming entrance.

If I have time, I like to give my workshop attendees a visual quiz with photos of a variety of rooms and ask them what elements they see. I have them point out some feng shui faux pas and/or areas that they like, and why. This is usually an audience hit as they love to show what they've learned. In conclusion, I leave all my audiences from every type of talk with some takeaway points and my "Top 10 Things-to-Do-When-You-Get-Home" list. (See Chapter 6 notes for my "Top 10" list.)

I have worked on this outline for a long time to create a flow of information that makes sense to someone new to the subject, and to those who want to take it further by reading a book, attending another workshop, or hiring me to consult about their space.

I invite my audience to give me their email address if they want more information on my services, and I offer to send them additional feng shui information as a gift. Without fail I give away a door prize.

Exercise: Draft a twenty-minute talk.

What are the building blocks of your work? Can you use them to describe what you do? Are you ready to give a twenty-minute talk to a local business group or group of friends? Practice!

(Don't forget to figure out a door prize!)

CHAPTER 7

Wealth & Prosperity A Flow of Gratitude	Fame & Reputation The Golden Rule in Action	Relationships Get to Know Your Clients
Health & Family You Are the Chief Health Officer	The Center Your Stable Base	Creativity Express Yourself and Connect with Others
Knowledge & Self-Cultivation Take Care of Yourself	Career & Journey How Do You Get to Where You Want to Go?	Helpful People & Travel Meet My Helpers

Relationships: Get to Know Your Clients

This chapter will discuss how I meet my clients and learn about them prior to their consultation. (Remember, I have been attracting them through my daily affirmations). I'll go over what I do in a residential/business consultation and a space blessing/clearing ceremony to give you some examples of what these relationships looks like. That's the "Hello" and "Getting to Know You" part; I also tell you how I handle "Good-bye."

Introduce Yourself and Invite Your Clients to Learn More

How are you going to meet your perfect clients? In the beginning, most likely via the web. Which means that you need a great website with search terms that will lead your clients to you. Once they arrive, invite them to connect and learn more. You can do that with a questionnaire. This feature on my website continues to be my most important marketing outreach tool.

People interested in learning more can fill it out and with an easy click can send it back directly from my website home page. Is it any wonder that I love this tool? Nearly 60 percent of my clients come from this process. The questionnaire gives people something to DO once they find me via the web, and it gets them thinking about why they would want to hire me. Here's the link: https://www.thrivingspaces.com/get-started/.

The questionnaire is simple and fast to complete and it's free. It asks how the respondent would like to be contacted—email, phone call or text—and I respond accordingly. Even if they don't become clients, my respondents have heard from me and know that I care and that I'm here. Will they be my perfect client? If they aren't, can I help them in some way to become more familiar with feng shui? Asking these questions has served me well over the years. Sometimes people show up later at a workshop or by contacting me when they're ready. (I recently worked with a client who contacted me again 10 months after her initial query.)

I am always excited to see a completed questionnaire in my email inbox. I have them color-coded so they pop on the screen. It's like a potential client saying "hello" with a knock on the door. Sometimes the query is a whisper of interest in feng shui and sometimes it's a cry for help. It's the start of a conversation I'm honored to be invited to have.

My questions are meant to be answered simply and quickly without having to be labored over. My first question is open-ended so people can respond to it however they want:

What would you like to gain, or receive, from a feng shui consultation?

Simple enough, but the answers are as diverse as the people who've written them and range from general to specific, neutral to personal, practical to spiritual. They always give me insight into the person asking me about feng shui. Here are some of the answers I've gotten to my first question.

- Abundance, joy, clarity, prosperity, and confidence
- Guidance
- More (and perfect) clients
- Better sleep!
- Health for the family, success, and harmony
- Good fortune, love, organization, comfort
- Help me sell my house
- Energy flow throughout
- A home that evokes peacefulness
- Paint colors before I move in
- I have a hard time unwinding and de-stressing at home

People write about leaving relationships and wanting to be open to new love. They write about wanting to attract money and creativity. Or about wanting children. They write about wanting to be purposeful and intentional with their spaces to help them reach their goals. They write about their health crises.

My next questions are specific about what is and what is not working in their lives. They ask specifically about areas of their lives that coincide with the Bagua areas in their homes or businesses. I give them a choice of three answers for each area:

1. Working well
2. Could use some help, but not critical
3. I want to make some changes NOW

When they answer that they want to make some changes NOW, I make a note to remind myself to look carefully at those areas in their home that correspond to the life areas they've told me they want to change. For example, if the respondent has an issue with their love relationship, when I'm in their home with them I'm going to be looking at the upper right corner (the Love & Marriage area of the Bagua grid) on their main floor and in each room, to see what's happening there.

The last questions I ask are what they love about their space and what they dislike about it, what their favorite and least favorite areas are and why. If I can help them resolve an issue about a least favorite area using the practical tools of feng shui while tapping into what they love about their favorite area, I can be a useful problem solver for them.

My respondents' answers have opened the door, but I haven't yet been invited into their lives. Though the questions I've asked are simple ones, I make sure I respond to each one with deep, honest answers. It is a profound moment when I receive such personal and privileged information, and I sit with it before answering. It is like standing on the virtual threshold of their home.

Now it's my turn to tell them a bit about me and how I can use my professional expertise to help them solve their issues. If we are a fit, I may get to stand on the actual threshold of their home or business and be invited in to share the power and practice of feng shui to guide the changes they want to make.

I try to send out a reply within a few hours of receiving a questionnaire. Most often, respondents want to be contacted by email, next by text, and last by phone. I answer every email query with a personal response to the issues they've spelled out.

I include it in a templated email paragraph with a sandwich-type format: top/first is my personal response to their specific issue/s, the middle section is a description of the service and how much it costs, and the bottom/last section contains information about my upcoming schedule and expresses gratitude for their interest. (See Chapter 1 notes for an example of how I use an email template.)

Exercise: Gather information about your clients.

How will you get information from potential clients before offering your services?

How will you invite visitors to request information or ask you a question?

Compose a templated paragraph that you can use to sandwich into an email response to a query.

Since 2017, in addition to residential and commercial consultations, I've offered space-clearing and blessing ceremonies with a particular focus on homes that are for sale. Along with vision board workshops, these are the sweet spots of my business, where I align what I love to do with what I believe clients need, want, and are so happy to receive. Since March 2020, I have been offering all my services online with remote consultations and remote workshops. Below are descriptions of these services:

Practice in Action: A Residential Feng Shui Consultation

I have refined what I do in a residential consultation after many years of trial and error, but you will want to create your own way of handling the time you spend with your clients.

Before each residential consultation, I:

- Speak to the client on the phone or by email. I usually have an idea of the main focus of the consultation and any particular issues they want to address from our conversation or their answers to my questionnaire. I make sure I have the correct spelling and pronunciation of their name/s, their email address, and mobile numbers. I ask who the appointment will be with and if there are partners or children who will be present. If the client has expressed an interest in paint colors, I make sure to pack my paint decks. If they have expressed an interest in purchasing new furniture, I sometimes check new trends or see if any local furniture outlets are having sales. If they have Pinterest boards, I ask if I can take a look at them. I always go over the questionnaire answers and my notes right before leaving for the appointment.

- Do a quick search for their name and map the location of their home. Often the home will show up on Realtor.com, Zillow, or Google Maps with a front view of the home and an aerial view as well. If the home has recently been sold, photos and a floor plan may be available. These will give me some important information, including whether the garage is attached or not, if there are any outbuildings on the lot, or if any buildings around the home or roadways are impinging on the energy around the home. I've usually gathered a lot of information about the home before I arrive.

- Pack my briefcase the night before the appointment with any handouts specific to the client's issues or concerns such as decluttering, feng shui practices for the landscape and garden, or holiday tips, if timely. I always include a printed Bagua and Five Elements chart and my client gift, the branded notepad. I bring extra business cards, pencils and pens, a tape measure, a paint sheen chart, my paint decks, a small personal notebook to make notes about follow-up, a red envelope to hold and energize their payment, and a snack!

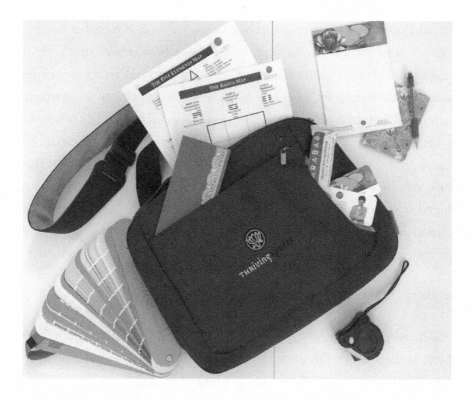

Figure 12 My packed briefcase. I'm ready to go!

- Write the name and contact information of my client and either leave it on the counter or email it to my husband. This is a good safety precaution for anyone doing consulting work in a client's home, particularly when you haven't met them yet.

Arrival – I try to get there exactly on time!

I always add ten to fifteen minutes to my drive time to make sure I arrive at the client's home on schedule. There are so many great navigation tools today that you can plan your arrival almost to the minute. I map the route before I go and write down the directions. I do this because I've been places where Siri was clueless as to where I was or the mapping software on my phone was simply wrong. When I arrive early, I can get an overview of the entire neighborhood, not just the street view from my phone.

I use the extra time to drive around the neighborhood to see what my client sees when they come home every day. I check how others are caring for their homes. And I look for the views—the good and the bad. Lastly, I note how easy it is to find the house. I have often talked to clients about moving their house numbers or changing them out because they are either too hard to see or too hard to read. Numbers arranged horizontally are the easiest to read. I try to arrive at the home "on the dot," even if I'm parked out front for a minute or two beforehand. In the past I have been too eager and shown up a little early but found that was irksome for some clients. I've learned since to leave my eagerness in the car, take a deep breath, and wait for the exact time of the appointment before I approach the front door.

Inside the home, the consultation begins after I say Hello!

Usually when I show up on a client's doorstep it is my first meeting with them. If they've been to my website, they will have a good idea of what I look like. If they are on Facebook or LinkedIn, I will have learned something about them, too. And though I may have spotted things on my way up the path or through the hallway to my client's door that I want to discuss with them, I don't start the consultation until after we've officially met and spent a few minutes together. We have an icebreaker conversation in which I give them their gift and tell them what we will be doing. I also give them the handouts I've selected for them, including a copy of the Bagua grid and the Five Elements chart. If they have a front and backyard, I give them my landscape tips; if they've already told me about issues they have with clutter, I give them a list of organizing tips. I remind them about the issues they brought up to me in our pre-consultation phone or email conversations so they know that I am truly present with them in their space and have a clear understanding of what they need.

This is my breathing time, too. A chance for me to take the pulse of the energy for a moment before walking around. Being present in the space with the owner I can pick up cues about their taste, such as the type of artwork they like, the colors they enjoy being around, their level of clutter, and the separation of public versus private spaces (e.g., if laundry is piled on the dining table there may not be a more logical space in the home to fold it). These first impressions help guide me as I walk through.

Before we walk around the home together, I remind the client of my two levels of service—one in which they take notes of my recommendations and the other in which I send them my recommendations in a written report. These services are priced differently; I charge an additional hour to create the report. My clients usually tell me in advance which one they want. But I also remind them they can change their minds and let me know at the end of the consultation if they do. I then ask their permission to take photos I can use to prepare their report or have on hand if they contact me with questions after the appointment.

We start at the front door.

After our icebreaker conversation, I head with the client back to the walkway leading to their entrance. I explain that the front door is the "mouth of chi," the place where energy enters the home. As forms of energy ourselves, we can sense when the entrance is welcoming. In Western culture, and particularly in parts of the country where neighborhoods have been designed and built around cars, most of us do not enter our homes from the front. We enter from our garages out back or at the side of the home. Sometimes the front areas can be forgotten or used only for guests. The feng shui elements I look for at the home's entrance have to do with safety: easy-to-find and readable house numbers; a clear, uncluttered path to the door; a welcome mat; and door hardware that works easily. I also look for signs of welcome and invitation: greeters in the form of plants, outdoor statues or furniture, and appropriate lighting. The entrance is a place where people can make easy changes: new house numbers if needed, a welcome mat if missing, plants, or better lighting. Usually I can give clients simple solutions and easy directions to help them enhance their "mouth of chi." This helps them to see that feng shui isn't too esoteric, strange, or expensive. Conversely, some clients already have beautiful, well-maintained pathways, safe lighting, and welcoming porches and front doors. It's a joy to tell them why everything they've done works so well from a safe, energetic, harmonious, and auspicious feng shui viewpoint.

Now we are ready to return inside.

Where to first?

Sometimes I begin my walk through the home from the front door or the foyer. Other times the client wants to head straight to the area that is bothering them or is the main issue in the space.

I prefer to begin in the "public" areas of the home—foyer, living room, dining room, and kitchen because, as an invited guest, I am still building rapport with my client and introducing myself to the home. These spaces are by nature less personal than is a bedroom, for example, and I can ask questions about furniture choices, artwork, and space usage so that the client can get an idea of how the consultation will proceed. We get comfortable being together, and they tell me about their lives through their stuff.

Imagine a dinner party where you are seated next to someone you don't know. The conversation may start with generalities—work, recent trips, family. You both display your public personas first. Later, if things are going well, one of you may learn about a recent recovery from knee surgery or how the other person's children like school. In the feng shui conversation we also share information from public to private—the conversation evolving as we move from public living spaces to private ones.

Most of my clients have a specific area in their space or issue in their lives that they have hired me to help them change. Of course, I want to address that space or issue during the consultation, but I also listen for other clues to help me identify any underlying dis-ease in the home. For example, I frequently find that clients have difficulty sleeping but seldom identify it as an issue until I (gently) ask about it. Getting a good's night sleep can positively impact everything in one's life, and I try to make suggestions to help my clients achieve it.

Another example is when I'm asked to help with a goal like attracting wealth. I may find out that the client has stifled their creativity by hiding their paintings in the basement or is not paying attention to their health by ignoring dirt and clutter in the home. Each of the Bagua areas impacts the others, just as aspects of our lives interconnect. So instead of heading right to the Wealth & Prosperity area of their home to see how they currently express abundance in their lives, I look at other areas of the Bagua and the elemental balance that exists or is missing throughout the home. In most feng shui consultations, I have found that all parts of the Bagua must be in sync to create the beautiful, harmonious whole, and, most importantly for the client, to help them reach their ultimate goal.

Here are the things I look for in every consultation as the client and I walk around their home:

- Missing areas of the Bagua. This is an area (or areas) that is/are missing from the home if you were looking at the floor plan and drew lines from all the outer walls to complete the shape of a rectangle. Often an attached garage that protrudes from the front or back of the home creates a missing area or areas beside it. This is not unusual in Western-designed homes and is often easily remedied with an anchoring "cure": planting a tree/bush where the lines meet, placing a statue, solar light, or bench where the "phantom" walls would meet.

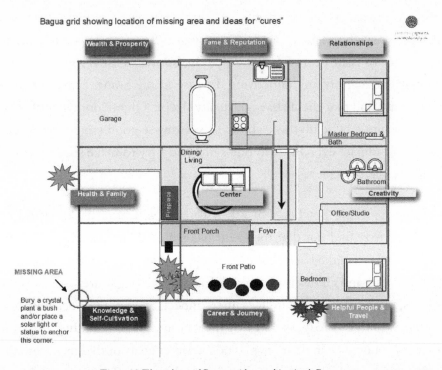

Figure 13 Floor plan and Bagua grid created in Apple Pages.

- Clutter and where it is located. I identify what the clutter may mean to the client based on where it is located. In feng shui, we say that clutter can result in stuck energy. Clutter in the Wealth & Prosperity area may suggest that the client's wealth is stuck—either not coming in or not growing. Clutter in the Love & Marriage area may suggest confusion about the relationship, overwhelming feelings, or an inability to resolve issues. Feng shui knowledge can help diagnose an issue based on where it falls inside the Bagua. Conversely, no clutter anywhere in a home, expressed as unadorned surfaces and walls, smooth floors without rugs, and few photos or personal items may suggest an imbalance of too much yang energy and might be an issue for the client.

- Elemental and yin and yang imbalance. I can problem solve why an area may be causing issues by looking at the elemental balance (or imbalance) in the space. For example, I had clients who loved their home, which they also worked from, but felt stuck financially in their business and in their personal lives. I noticed that their front door and foyer, located in the Center area of the Bagua, had a low, built-in fountain, next to a wall with dark wallpaper. I quickly ascertained that we had Water elemental energy mixing with Earth elemental energy—resulting in a big elemental "mud" problem (Earth and Water Elements mixed together) that was creating a lot of stuck energy. Once the clients changed out this area with new white and silver wallpaper (colors that express the Metal Element and balance the Earth Element) and eliminated the water feature, they began to feel better and their business took off.

- Artwork. This is one of my favorite conversations to have with clients: what their artwork means to them and why they've placed it where they have. I often will recommend moving or removing art that may be creating problems where it's placed. For example, I had a client who had a photo of a skeletal man in an impoverished desert village in their Wealth & Prosperity area. One of the issues they asked me to help them with was the feeling of lack in their lives and how they could bring in more money. They had placed a visual expression of lack of food and other basics in the area of their home that is aligned with abundance. I recommended they move that piece of art.[9]

- Mirrors! One of my feng shui teachers called mirrors the "aspirin" of feng shui. They can be a "cure" for many environmental ailments and used in many ways to change out the energy of a space. Mirrors represent the Water Element, which expresses the energy of flow and deep feelings. Mirrors can move and bounce light (energy) around a space. They can literally place us in a space that helps us to feel present. When a room lacks energy, a mirror can often help enliven it. Mirrors can expand energy and even extend it to another Bagua area.

_____

[9] You might wonder where art like this could go. It happened to be a photo that the client had taken while traveling and he was proud of the story it told. He put it in the Creativity area of his home to highlight his craft.

- Plants. Most of my clients love plants. Live plants bring oxygen into the home, bringing a breath of fresh air to a space. Their foliage can offer softness (yin) to the hard surface of a counter (yang) or fill in a corner to round out an angle. Grouped together they can bring abundance to the Wealth & Prosperity area. A heart-shaped pot with red, white, or pink flowers can bring romantic energy to the Love & Marriage corner. A variety of plants in different kinds of pots can enhance almost any area of the Bagua. I say almost, as an overabundance of plants placed in the center of the home can be destabilizing. This is because the Wood Element (expressed in the plants) consumes the Earth Element, which aligns with the Bagua Center. But the decision whether to add this element depends upon the client and their needs. In a circumstance where the client is feeling too grounded and wants to shake things up, plants in the Bagua Center of their home might just be the perfect cure.

- Furniture placement in the power or command position. I look for placement of the beds with the headboard placed against a solid wall, where the sleeper can see the door and any windows when lying in bed. This position makes us feel safe so we can turn our brains off and go to sleep. The same kind of placement works best for a desk in a home office (or any workspace). I recommend that the desk be placed with a solid wall behind it so that when the worker is seated at their desk, they have a clear view of the door and any windows in the space. This prevents any surprises coming through the door or past the windows that interrupt their focus.

- Storage areas, particularly the garage. Most of my clients don't really comprehend that their garages—if attached—are part of their homes. Garages are storage for cars and all the stuff we don't know what to do with. If they are attached to the home, they are energetically a part of the overall Bagua. I am prepared with ideas on how to enhance this area, just as I am for any other area of the Bagua. One thing I always look for when a single person wants to attract and invite another person into their lives is room in the garage for their new partner to park. I often find one car and the other space filled with stuff. Here's what else I look for in a garage:

o Room for cars and for people to move easily into and out of them

o Items up off the floor, allowing energy to flow around them. (Plus, the stuff is no longer metaphorically "beneath you" to deal with.)

o Enough storage shelving or space to easily access what is being stored

o Enough light to see

o Doors to the home and/or to the outside that open and close smoothly and fully (nothing stored behind them)

o Secure and clean windows

o A welcoming path and steps from the garage to home

If there's time, we look at the landscape and both the front and backyards of the home.

After almost two hours I find that my clients are tired and that it's time to stop and summarize. If they don't want a report, I help them prioritize the recommendations I've made. Sometimes I don't have an easy answer or recommendation for a particular issue "on the spot." If that happens, I tell them I need time to think more about it and will get back to them. This takes the pressure off me in the moment and allows creativity to flow again later, which it always does. I go over any follow-up steps I'll take, such as sending them paint sheet samples or links to resources related to ideas we discussed. I leave enough time to go through the payment "ceremony" with the red envelope and thank them for inviting me in. This "ceremony" at the conclusion of our appointment is usually profound for me and for my clients.

Exercise: What will you cover in your consultation?

Make a checklist of what you want to bring to your consultation and what areas you want to cover with your client. A checklist will help you stay focused on the important things you want to discuss and keep you on track should you get waylaid in a particular area of the home.

Practice in Action: A Business Consultation

One of the biggest differences between a residential and a business consultation is that business clients want to get down to business! Businesspeople are usually very clear about what they need, so there is less probing on my part to get to the nut of what we're trying to crack in the form of creating change. They usually contact me for the following reasons:

- They are moving offices and need help with the arrangement in a different space.

- They are creating new spaces for everyone, so they need help with floor plan design, wall and interior window placement, community and training areas, and the selection of appropriate artwork.

- They are looking for energy flow to create wealth and growth.

For a business located in a commercial building, there usually isn't a lot that can be done on the outside to attract energy to the business inside. I look for ease in finding them in the first place (money equals energy in this equation, and I want to make sure my client's business is easily found, whether they see clients or customers in the space or not). Certainly, I will make recommendations if I think there is a safety issue that should be addressed, but I don't spend a lot of time on the outside of large commercial buildings, as my clients don't usually have any input there.

110

I look at the lobby to make sure it is welcoming and that there is good signage for the business I'm visiting. I look through my "feng shui" eyes at the elevator, the hallway, and the door to their offices as well. Lobby signage is something that my clients who rent or lease space may have some input on with the building management. Having their name on the door is important.

Just as in a residential appointment, I like to sit down with my client for a moment to absorb the energy of the office and meet anyone who has come along with us for the consult. It's important in this initial meeting to ascertain who the decision-maker is in the group; sometimes it's not the person who set up the meeting! Once everyone is gathered, I make sure that I understand the priorities for the consult and share my thoughts on the building entrance and lobby area.

With most of my business clients, the focus is on wealth building and market reach—the Wealth & Prosperity, Fame & Reputation, and Helpful People & Travel areas of the Bagua are often priorities. I explain that we'll be looking at all Bagua areas, but that I like to start with their lobby or foyer, the first space their customers see. It is here that I talk about the need for:

- A clear message to customers about what to do as they enter the space, particularly if there is no receptionist (as can be the case for small offices).

- A safe, comfortable area for their customers to wait in.

- Signage that says the customer is in the right place at the right time (a simple message board with the business name on it or a "We'll be with you in a moment" from the receptionist lets them know this).

- Something for customers to do while waiting—magazines, a TV on, music playing.

- Water or the makings for tea or coffee, or a dish of candy or bowl of snacks.

Here are other issues I usually need to address in a commercial consultation:

Are there spaces for all their needs?

- In a family and children's therapist's office, I'll check for comfortable chairs for all sizes of adults and kids, and waiting room magazines and accessories appropriate for the ages of the clients being seen. I recommend a mirror in the entry of a therapist's office so that everyone who arrives can literally "see" themselves in the space. This is particularly appropriate for children.

- In a business office, I'll look for places to pause and rest, as there are usually lots of places to work. I'll look for areas where employees can rest their eyes as well as their bodies—a community space or kitchen that is not cluttered and hopefully not also used for storing office supplies. I often recommend a bulletin board for employees to announce important events in their lives or post photos.

- In the storage area of a business, I'll look for clutter and remind the client that clutter represents stuck energy and can negatively impact their bottom line! Storage areas are often places that attract junk no one knows what to do with. Business owners are often surprised to learn that their closets and storage spaces are part of their Bagua—and their business energy. Sometimes commercial buildings have storage areas that are included in the lease. I ask the owner to check to see if that's an option. Almost all businesses need coat racks, especially if they use their coat closets for other storage. Sometimes all that is needed are hooks on the backs of doors or along a wall in a community area.

- In retail spaces, I look at yin and yang balance (whether there is enough space/too much space between the objects on display), cash register placement, decoration in the changing rooms, lighting, sound, and scent. Have you ever walked into a shop and then turned around and left? I have when I've felt there was something literally pushing me back out—it could be an overwhelming scent (I'm very sensitive to this as are others), an overabundance of merchandise (which overwhelms and confuses me before I even begin to look around), loud or disruptive music or lighting. A space that is too dark usually doesn't feel safe. Of course, it could be that I'm not the retail shop's perfect customer, but if I am their feng shui consultant, I'll want to know their definition of the perfect customer before I help them make changes.

Where is the desk?

- In many offices I visit, desks are facing the walls. If there is room, I show my clients how to set their desks up in the power or command position—facing outward with a solid wall behind them so they can see the door and windows. If there isn't room to change the position of the desk, I recommend a mirror cure. See next bullet point.

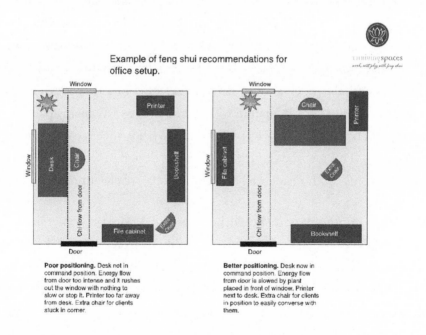

Figure 14 An example of how to move furniture so the desk is in the "power" or "command" position.

- In an office cubicle where it isn't possible to move the desk into the command or power position, I show the client how a small mirror, affixed to the wall that their desk faces, allows the worker to see what is behind them, by glancing in the mirror, without turning their neck.

- I ask if headphones are an option for cubicle workers. Wearing headphones at one's desk is an easy way to signal that a worker doesn't want to be disturbed. For workers who are introverts or have a problem focusing, noise-canceling headphones can be very helpful.

- For offices where most of the workers are in cubicles, I ask if there are private spaces where people can make phone calls or occasionally work with a door closed on a temporary basis. Usually there is a space that can be allocated for this type of work.

Most businesses can express their unique purpose and personality through paint color. I recommend color based on the Five Elements associated with their Bagua grid, the nature of the business, whom the business wants to attract, and the colors the business owners are drawn to. I try to give lots of examples and always encourage them to select colors they love. You can create an account with Benjamin Moore and Sherwin Williams paint companies which will allow you to send 8" x 10" paint sheet color samples to your clients. This is a free service they offer to design professionals and one that my clients, both residential and commercial, really appreciate.

Lighting is important and should be intentional. Most commercial office buildings have some sort of overhead lighting. I recommend LED over fluorescent fixtures because they are more energy efficient and easier on the eyes when working. I remind clients to have different kinds of light in the office—task lighting in group work areas, undercounter lighting in community kitchens, and desk lighting for workers who prefer softer light and don't want the overheads on at all.

I almost always recommend plants for offices—they clean the air, soften corners, and bring color and life into the space. There are lots of great articles about the best plants for indoor office spaces based on the natural or artificial light that is available. I recommend plants without sharp, pointed leaves that might poke or snag fabric. I don't recommend live plants for health care spaces as some people have allergies. Silk or artificial plants are great in these spaces.

Finally, I review ways to minimize the hazards of working constantly around a lot of electronics and attempt to help office workers hide or corral cords. If a client is in the build-out phase, I recommend that they ask for plenty of outlets (to minimize overloading any one outlet) and that they be strategically placed to avoid having to use extension cords, which can become a tripping hazard. Plants help clean the air of electromagnetic emissions, as do salt lamps.

My commercial appointments are usually two hours long. I leave enough time to summarize and make sure I've covered the issues the client has asked about. If more time is needed, we schedule another appointment. My commercial clients often want a PayPal or email invoice, which I send when I return to my office.

I always write a thank you note to everyone who was with me during the consultation.

Practice in Action: Remote Consultations

I offer remote consultations as a way to serve clients outside of my service area[10]. I appreciate clients willing to work with me remotely, to trust that I'll be able to clearly visualize their space via floor plan drawings, photos, and videos, and that I'll understand how the energy flows during our walk-

---

[10] During the Covid-19 pandemic stay-at-home and safer-at-home restrictions, I offered remote consultations and video workshops within my service area, too.

through via applications like FaceTime, Zoom, Skype, and What's App. There are ways to make the process as productive and creative as being together in a live consultation. This is because I have reviewed the floor plan and seen the space through my client's eyes from the videos and photos I ask them to send ahead of the consultation. This is material I don't usually have prior to a live consult. While I still offer recommendations during our virtual walk-through, I have a list of recommendations I've prepared for them before we begin. I've found there is less small talk during a virtual visit, which often leads to a very efficient and focused consultation. In the beginning of my practice, I felt that remote consultations took second place to a live consult, but now, with more experience and fine-tuning, I believe they are equally beneficial. Getting comfortable and confident doing remote consultations is another way to continue to serve our clients near and far.

Here's what I've found works best:

- The client fills in the questionnaire on my website, so I know their goals and the issues they want to address. (This is no different than what is done for a typical live consultation.)

- We communicate by phone or email so I can describe the preparation process. We determine the scope of the work and set our "appointment" based on an agreed technology for their mobile phones or tablets. Working with a handheld device with a front- and back-facing camera works best.

- The client digitally sends me their floor plan (either a scan of a hand-drawn plan or of architectural plans), photos of the space and/or videos, preferably both. I've found that a series of short videos (walking to their front door and into each of their rooms, for example) works best so I can easily re-watch the short segments where I need help understanding the floor plan flow. Sending the videos via Dropbox or other file-sharing service works best because these files are usually quite large.

- I review the floor plan, photos and videos, and then draw and send the Bagua in advance, along with any questions I have about the space. I make notes for recommendations, as I will have already been thinking about their space and how I can help them.

- We hold our scheduled video call on a phone or tablet, and we "walk" together through the space just as we would in a live consultation. The client may choose to record our conversation, stop and take notes along the way, or have me write up a report. We determine a future time for me to check back with them.

- I request electronic payment for service at the end of the appointment.

Exercise: What are your services?

What are your services or levels of service and how are they alike and different?

Would having a list of what you do during each consultation or for each service help you? If so, make a list of the things you don't want to forget to do for each type of appointment.

Do you provide handouts for each type of service? If so, keep them in a file on your computer for easy access and print them out when you need them.

Find Your Sweet Spot and Grow Your Business

In the beginning of your practice you probably won't know where the sweet spot is. I'm talking about the service you provide that makes you so happy you don't feel like you're working and makes your clients so happy they are ready, eager, and grateful to pay you. That is being in and living your creativity!

Your sweet spot could be:

- Doing consultations for homeowners
- Doing consultations for business owners
- Doing consultations for landscape gardeners
- Leading workshops
- Speaking at special events
- Writing blogs and e-books
- Creating online workshops
- Coaching clients
- Creating products for your clients to buy
- Teaching feng shui through a local continuing ed college or service
- Selecting artwork for clients based on their Bagua and elemental enhancement needs
- Offering space-clearing, house-blessing, and farewell ceremonies
- Offering decluttering and organizing services
- And, many more ideas!

Whatever it is, finding it may take time, but I'm confident you will. Finding what you love to do means being aware of where you shine and where you have a million ideas to share. Conversely, there may be areas of feng shui you shy away from because you do not feel as confident about them as you do other areas (always good to note!) but may also not have as much desire to learn about. Remember one of the general tenets of feng shui—nonjudgment—of spaces, of clients. We need to offer the generosity of nonjudgment to ourselves, too. There will be aspects of the feng shui practice you will love, and others that you won't. Finding out which is which is part of becoming a great practitioner. Marketing your sweet spot service/s will help you grow your business because you will love providing them, people will love receiving them, and they will tell others about them or send you testimonials about their results.

Here is how I found one of mine:

I was happily offering a range of services I thought feng shui practitioners provided: home, business, and landscape consultations. I found out pretty quickly that I wasn't as good at landscape consultations as I was at home and/or business consults. I wasn't terrible at it—in fact, I enjoyed giving folks general information about the best place for their water feature or their fire pit; the kid's play equipment or color for plants, bushes, and ceramic pots; or where to hang those two cute birdhouses. What I found was that most clients seeking feng shui landscaping advice really wanted help with choosing the right plants, bushes, and trees. I am most certainly not a landscape designer with vast plant and soil knowledge, and I could not give my clients what they really wanted in a landscape consultation. Offering this type of consultation on my website didn't tick my integrity box because I didn't feel that I was giving my clients great value with this service. So, I deleted landscape consultations from my website. As feng shui practitioners, we know what happens when we remove something, right? We make room for something new.

Which is exactly what happened to me. I had a realtor friend ask me for help with a condo listing that wasn't selling. The condo was empty, and her client was getting antsy because there hadn't been any showings. My friend said the condo was priced right, but she didn't know what else she could do. She wondered if feng shui could help. I told her, yes, feng shui could help if her client was open to saying good-bye to the condo, thanking it for sheltering her, and welcoming new homeowners to enjoy it. Her client was skeptical but willing and followed my instructions. They had a showing and contract within a week.

I had shied away from working with realtors because I thought it meant offering feng shui staging. I didn't want to have staging materials on hand to loan to clients or spend time moving furniture around for staging. However, I love helping people understand that the relationship with their home changes when they list it for sale and to help them through the process of saying thank you and good-bye to it. I thought this could be a new service for me: creating farewell and blessing ceremonies for homeowners listing their homes.

To feel confident about offering this service, I took an online course on elemental space clearing through the WSFS, re-read Denise Linn's fabulous *Sacred Spaces* (she also teaches courses), and provided complimentary ceremonies to several friends, who had great success selling their homes quickly, in one instance the following day! I felt ready to begin offering this service in 2018. A farewell and blessing ceremony is a powerful, personal, and emotional event, and I am profoundly honored to offer this service. It not only is a sweet spot for me to be a helpful person in the world, but also a very sweet time to spend with clients in a tender moment of their lives.

Although you may be good at something, you still have to codify what it is you are doing and make sure that what you offer is of value to your clients and can be replicated. Here is what creating and presenting farewell and blessing ceremonies entails for me:

- It takes me about an hour and a half to two hours to prepare and implement the ceremony: thirty to forty-five minutes of prep phone call and script writing and thirty to sixty minutes for the ceremony in the home, where I walk through with the owners and introduce myself to the home, hear some stories about the owners' lives in the home, and then sit with them to hold the "service."

- I create and bring a simple centerpiece that includes the feng shui Five Elements for the group to sit around. Typically, I bring a ceramic (Earth Element) bowl or platter filled with water (Water Element) and floating herbs or flowers (Wood Element) with white, round (Metal Element) candles (Fire Element). I invite the clients to add anything they'd like to personalize the centerpiece– flowers, a special photo or statue, toys from the kids, even books. To date, this has rarely happened. The clients are always glad I have brought a centerpiece with me. It's nice to have something to focus on while presenting and leading the ceremony.

- I make copies of the script for everyone attending.

- I light the candles at the beginning of the ceremony. I bring a Bic or Zippo-type lighter so I won't have burned matches to pick up and the candles can be lit on the first try! When the ceremony is over, I ask the clients to blow out the candles. When children are involved in the ceremony, I make sure they each have a candle to blow out.

Figure 15 An example of a blessing ceremony centerpiece.

This has been a great service for me to offer to realtors and home sellers. Saying good-bye to a home can be hard, even if there are so many happy reasons to be moving into a new one! I have not done one of these ceremonies without tears—the clients' and mine. And that, to me, is sweet.

Exercise: Find your sweet spots.

What do you love to do? These are your sweet spots. Think about your favorite parts of providing services to your clients. For example, maybe it's helping them pick paint colors or organizing their pantries or closets. Both these activities come up during a feng shui consultation and could become more in-depth services for you. Also, you could deepen your knowledge with additional coursework and certification in both those areas should you choose. You catch my drift here; look closely at what you love to do and find out if it is another option for deepening and perfecting your craft and practice, while offering additional value to your clients.

Saying Good-Bye: To Hug or Not to Hug

Not everyone enjoys or welcomes the physical connection of a hug, but I can usually tell if someone is open to it or not. There is a closeness that develops in the short time I have with clients, and they often ask if they can hug me good-bye! I am a hugger, so this is an easy one for me. It may not be for you, and you should be ready with an alternative way of connecting. A warm handshake is great. There are hugging exceptions, of course: I don't hug my male clients good-bye. Sadly, in today's world, hugs can be taken the wrong way and I don't want there ever to be any uncomfortable energy at the end of a great feng shui consultation. I stick out my hand enthusiastically and smile. It's important to end your consultation on a high note, so decide in advance how you want to handle parting with your client.

CHAPTER 8

Wealth & Prosperity	Fame & Reputation	Relationships
A Flow of Gratitude	The Golden Rule in Action	Get to Know Your Clients
Health & Family	**The Center**	**Creativity**
You Are the Chief Health Officer	Your Stable Base	Express Yourself and Connect with Others
Knowledge & Self-Cultivation	**Career & Journey**	**Helpful People & Travel**
Take Care of Yourself	How Do You Get to Where You Want to Go?	Meet My Helpers

Creativity: Express Yourself and Connect with Others

Your marketing is an expression of you and your work. It is your chance to connect with others in a way that shares your gifts of service and/or product. You are the creator, producer, designer, and communicator for your business. Think of marketing as a pleasant conversation in which you share information and make a connection. As in any conversation, there is talking (push) and listening (pull.) You and your clients or customers will do both; to be successful, you need both. (I discuss the definition of push and pull marketing, and their hybrids, in Chapter 4.) Your marketing should express your brand, which actually is YOU. Have some fun with it and let it express your style in the world. Below I list the tools I use, the ones I don't, and the mistakes I've made so you can learn from them.

The Family of Marketing Tools I Love and Use

Website. This is the most important marketing tool you have. Your emails, your business card, and your workshops—all of the products and activities you create to sustain your work—should lead people back to your website, where they can learn more about you, read testimonials, buy and receive a service or product from you, and find out what you're up to next. Your website is working for you all the time. I have received emailed questionnaires that clocked in at 2 a.m., so make sure your website is virus-free, up to date with all its software, and has no broken links. Hire someone to help you if you don't want to be in charge of its overall health.

Professional photo that looks like you, today. Use the same photo everywhere you market yourself—on your website, your business card, your Facebook business page (or personal page, if that's what you choose), on your LinkedIn, Instagram, and Pinterest profiles, and anywhere anyone can find you on the web. You want consistency and professionalism. Do NOT show up at someone's home looking different than your photo; they will be confused. And confused people aren't happy people. Update your photo as needed.

Business cards. Make your business cards engaging and fun, beautiful to the touch, easy to read and understand, and expressive of who you are. Pass them out wherever you go. Leave some with your massage therapist, your yoga studio, your friendly librarian, your hairdresser—everybody. Always have some with you. I LOVE business cards, my own and other people's!

Email marketing subscription platforms. These web-based platforms are your worker bees, so learn all about them and build your email list. With one of these subscriptions you can send a large-batch email message that won't get blocked. A message sent using regular email with a bcc will often get blocked if it contains over fifty addresses. Also, regular email can't always support the graphics in your message (photos, videos, or illustrations). A subscription email marketing platform allows you to send thoughtful, value-filled, clever, fun, and interesting information to clients who have signed up to receive it.

I have used both Constant Contact and Mailchimp email marketing sub-scription platforms. My paid Constant Contact subscription gave me unlimited access to telephone customer service help—a boon in the begin-ning as I was learning how to use the service. Constant Contact subscription prices are based on the number of email subscribers you have. As I became more adept and added subscribers, I switched to Mailchimp, which offers a free service with a larger number of email subscribers. This was cheaper for me, and because I knew how these programs worked, I could switch to the free service and have more subscribers. Mailchimp also has a paid service that offers telephone support. Whichever service you choose, I recommend paying for online and telephone support in the beginning.

Social media. I think of social media as both push and pull marketing—you create a presence and populate that presence with information, news, events, photos, and quotes to push your message out. Then people find you on your social media platforms (pull).

This doesn't have to take over your time or your life. You get to select which platforms you want—Facebook, Pinterest, and LinkedIn are the ones I use. I chose to have a Facebook for Business page because I wanted to separate my *personal* Facebook presence, where I share information with family and friends, from my *business* Facebook presence, where I share information about Thriving Spaces and my work. Both types of Facebook pages allow you to post information, videos, and photos to share either privately or publicly. I keep my business Facebook page public and my personal page private. One of my feng shui sisters gave me a great idea to bridge the two: create a post for my Facebook for Business page and then share it on my personal page. (Thanks, Lisa!)

LinkedIn is a social networking platform that's all about business and networking. It's a great place to share my blog posts, events, and workshops, and to demonstrate credibility and build brand awareness.

Pinterest is a social media website that allows you to organize and share images and videos by "pinning" them to an online "bulletin board." I use this site to create feng shui pin boards that I can send clients to explain a feng shui concept or design idea. One of my favorite Pinterest links is to clever (and inexpensive) ways to cover mirrored closet doors. Also, Pinterest is helpful when clients have their own themed boards I can look at to give me a visual depiction of what they want to achieve in their spaces.

Digital marketing tools. There are many web-based business applications to choose from, and most have complimentary versions which I gratefully use unless I need the additional services in the paid subscription. Here are my favorites:

- Canva – I use the free version, but there is a Canva for Business that has more photos and design tools. I create Facebook covers, blog post graphics, postcards, email campaigns, invitations, and more. Easy and fun!

- Dropbox – a great file-sharing tool, particularly when clients want to share large design files or videos with me. I use the free version, but the paid subscription version has a lot more storage.

- Google Analytics – a free tool to see how people use your website, which keywords people use to find you, and which pages they go to and spend time on.

- Payment platforms: Venmo currently is free to use to receive and request payment when funded with a Venmo balance, bank account, or debit card. PayPal charges a service fee for each invoice paid and allows you to brand and describe your service when requesting payment. E-junkie, with a monthly fee, can be branded, too, and has an automatic thank you email you can customize in response.

- Remote consultation video platforms: FaceTime comes with my iPhone; Skype, What's App, and Google Meet can be used on your phone or your computer. All are free to use when you create an account. I also use Zoom for remote consults.

- Zoom – I used this only occasionally before Covid-19 but now I use it all the time for meetings and workshops. I have the subscription service so I can have additional security, see and respond to questions in a chat box, and have unlimited time for meetings.

- Survey Monkey – I have the free version of this application and use it to send out surveys after workshops and sometimes in my email campaigns.

Notepads or other branded gifts. There are notepad companies out there that will design a notepad for you using your logo, brand colors, and type. I designed my own using Canva. Most printing companies also have a promotional arm that can customize anything from mugs to T-shirts to sunscreen and hand lotion. A well-chosen book, crystal, or candle would also make a lovely gift. Remember your brand and what you stand for as you create your special gift. As a feng shui professional, I want to make sure I don't add to someone's clutter.

Networking memberships and directories. I have connected with new clients from participating in the organizations I belong to and taking the time to create and update my directory listing. Create a listing for your business in your feng shui school directory (that's a no-brainer!). I also belong to two paid membership business organizations, the Lowry Business Alliance (my neighborhood business group), and the International Feng Shui Guild. Both of these networking groups offer a directory listing, which is a great benefit. Each organization will have a different way of showcasing their members. This could include uploading photos and videos, including your headshot, adding your bio and testimonials, and answering a list of questions. Do it and then update it periodically to refresh the energy.

Thank you notes. You may decide that you don't need to print up your own professional thank you notecards, but I recommend that you do. It's another way to convey your gratitude within your brand. The important thing is to send them out. An actual card, written by hand and sent in the mail, is a graceful gesture in a world sorely in need of such courtesies.

Figure 16 My thank you note is branded to match my website and includes my logo.

Speaking engagements and workshops. These are powerful marketing tools and embrace both push and pull marketing. If it's a public event, a library program for example, you will send (push) out an email to your email subscriber list announcing it. The program provider will also publicize (push) the event. Have a catchy title for your talk and post it on your social media and website. Also write about it in a blog post so people can find it (pull) with their own search.

What's the difference between a speaking engagement and a workshop? For me, a speaking engagement is an invitation to speak about a particular topic, usually for an hour or less. It can be a paid function or complimentary. A workshop is usually longer—mine are up to three hours—and includes tasks for the attendees to complete: drawing their own Bagua on their floor plan or making a vision board, for example. These are almost always paid affairs, unless I'm doing one as a give-back gift to a charitable organization.

Speaking is an excellent way to meet people, get your brand message across, and share your expertise in service to the public and your potential clients. Start small and offer to speak for free until you feel ready to add it as a professional paid service.

Here is what I currently offer:

- A complimentary, twenty-minute talk on feng shui for professional groups, individual book groups, garden clubs, realtors, or anyone who is interested. In the beginning, these talks didn't result in new client queries, but now I envision perfect clients in the audience and this level of visualization has resulted in new business or a new opportunity every time. For me, this twenty-minute talk is more conversational than a formal presentation, and I've given them in a living room, office building lobby, and small conference room.

- Paid speaking engagements. These are usually one-hour programs with time for Q & A at the end. I have created the following presentations with accompanying PowerPoint slides for a variety of groups.
    - o Introduction to Feng Shui
    - o Feng Shui in the Garden
    - o Feng Shui Tips to Refresh Your Home for Spring
    - o Feng Shui in the Bedroom: Rest, Reconnect, and Rejuvenate
    - o Feng Shui Staging Techniques for Home Sellers

- o   Feng Shui for the Holidays

- o   Feng Shui for Prosperity

- o   Feng Shui Staging (for realtors)

- o   Feng Shui for Business Prosperity

- "Understanding the Feng Shui Bagua: Your Life's Eight "Treasures" Mapped Out on Your Floor Plan." This is a two-hour workshop with an introduction to feng shui first, then a hands-on drawing exercise afterward.

- Vision Board workshop. This is a three-hour, hands-on workshop I create, market, and present, usually in January and February, using feng shui organization tools to help attendees envision their futures and honor the many aspects of their lives. I have been conducting these workshops since 2014, and they have become a big part of my business at the beginning of the year. I do public workshops and private ones for realtors, community groups, and other organizations. I recently created an online version of this workshop as well.

Sign-up forms (printed and email). At my speaking engagements I supply printed sign-up forms (on colored paper) for audience members to return to me with their names and email addresses if they are interested in a follow-up consultation, a workshop, a space blessing, speaking engagement, or just want to be added to my mailing list. If I'm speaking to a large group, I put the forms on their chairs before the event. For a smaller group, I either pass out the forms or set them in a spot where they can be picked up at the end. When a form is returned to me, I send back a gift via email—a special Bagua I have created or a list of tips for the season. My email gift changes.

I often take some custom notepads to speaking engagements to use as door prizes. During the Q & A, I ask a volunteer to pass around a bag or box for people to place their form or business card inside. I usually ask a member of the audience or the host/hostess of the event to draw the winning name/s. I also have a link to this contact information form in my Mailchimp email signature.

Video. One of the tips I learned about creating videos is to write your (video) story in six words. Think about the genre of your video in terms of Hollywood films (horror, sci-fi, romantic comedy, drama, etc.) and then come up with your story. This is a film school exercise. What a great way to get your creative juices flowing! My first six-word story about feng shui was: *Moved couch. Got raise. Found soulmate.*

Did you know that 85 percent of people who watch videos don't turn on the sound? I did not. It is best to caption any video you make. Rev.com will transcribe and caption your video for about $1/word. Be sure to have a progress bar, as some people won't open a video unless they know in advance how long it is. (That would be me.)

After you've made your video, you will need to have it "hosted." The easiest way to do this is to upload it to a YouTube channel you can create for free. From there you can send the YouTube link in an individual email, post it on your blog, social media platform, or your website, or use it to illustrate a point in an email campaign.

Online workshops or webinars. Many platforms are available for hosting your workshop or webinar, and it's really up to you to find the one with the features you want at the price that makes sense for your business. If you have a workshop or class you enjoy teaching live, you may want to think about teaching the same class online. I started with Ruzuku and have moved to Zoom. Check out Udemy, Teachable, Creative Live, MasterClass, and others. Before choosing, I would take a class with one of them to see if you like their platform for learning.

Text. I have found that more and more clients want to communicate by text. This has been challenging for me because I don't like to type anything too long or complex on my phone screen, such as a description of my services and prices. Some computer applications, such as iMessage on Apple computers, sync with iPhones and iPads so you can type your message on your computer or tablet and send it as a text. Samsung and Apple have voice-to-text features on their recent models, which also make communicating by text easier. I have a colleague who is a master at this, but it takes practice, people! Always check for misspellings, autocorrect "fails," and punctuation mistakes, which sometimes make reading texts confounding (and make you look like an idiot!). I don't send emojis on business texts. I often draft and send a client text to myself first and read it *on my phone* to check for typos, clarity, and length before copying and sending it on to them.

Phone call. I telephone people if they ask me to on their questionnaire, as a callback to a voicemail, or by appointment. I love having a voice conversation with someone about how my work could help them, but with the increasing influx of robocalls, I don't answer my phone when I don't recognize the number. Create a welcoming voicemail message for anyone calling and willing to leave their information, then prepare for and enjoy the callback.

Marketing Tools I Do NOT Use

Printed flyers or brochures. In my first year in business, I created a postcard brochure with a beautiful photo collage on the front and information about feng shui and my business on the back. People loved it, but I got very little business out of the process. The brochure was fun to create but, alas, there was no return on investment (ROI). You are investing your time, in addition to your money, in making your business a viable entity, however you define that. Be aware of your ROI so that you make smart decisions. Some folks like to have a printed brochure, but I consider my website, my Facebook page, my Pinterest page, and my blog as my "brochure." It's published, just not printed. You—and your budget—get to decide which way you want to go.

Advertising. I once paid for a beautiful (in my opinion) ad in a local newsletter (distributed free to 5,000 neighbors) for six months and got one call from someone who didn't want to pay for my services. It wasn't a large investment of money and ultimately was a good learning experience, but I learned that this was not how I wanted to spend my marketing money. I wrote a column for the same newsletter which helped me become recognized as a feng shui expert in the neighborhood. I wasn't paid to write it, so it cost me time, but I could trace three clients who found me through that column. It was a much better use of my time (which, when you are a consultant, is also money).

I tried Google Ads, the free offer that came in the mail for $100 worth of advertising. This is an opt-out service that you have to remember to turn off or you'll get charged. I forgot and I did get charged. Again, I paid for advertising (which could have been totally free had I been paying attention) that I could not trace to any client connections. There may be some type of advertising that makes sense to you. If so, I encourage you to try a small investment in one and see what happens.

I think of the marketing budget as a percentage of income. The larger the income you set as a goal, the larger your marketing will need to be to achieve that goal. When setting up your business, you will need to invest more money in getting the word out about what you do—creating a website, professional photos and graphics, purchasing business cards, thank you cards and gifts, and enrolling in email or other electronic service subscriptions. Once set up, though, you can do a lot of marketing yourself—writing blog entries, posting to your social media, writing articles for local newsletters, speaking at your local library or other groups, creating and posting videos. All marketing is having the courage to tell your story so you can be out in the world sharing your services and products.

> *Exercise: Pick some marketing tools you'll use.*
>
> *Think about all the marketing tools out there and make a list of those that sound like*
>
> A. *They'll work for you and your budget.*
> B. *They sound fun to you, e.g., you will enjoy creating or implementing them.*
> C. *How you will know if they're working for you.*

Mistakes I've Made (So You Don't Have To)

If you want to be in business, revel in all it has to teach you, and reap the rewards of your successes, you have to let loose and fail sometimes. Here are my top-10 fails and what I learned from them:

1. **Storing client data in paper folders.** In my first weeks in business, I created red paper file folders for each client. I printed out relevant emails and reports and placed them in a file cabinet. It only took about a month before I got behind in creating these files. Then, I just stopped doing it. My advice: Don't even start with paper files. Just keep all relevant information—graphics, emails, reports—in client folders on your computer.

2. **Sending hard copy reports.** I sent out hard copy reports in beautiful red folders. Email reports are smarter (you can send links to photos and websites, which clients LOVE), faster (no waiting in line at the post office), and cheaper (no postage). Nuff said.

3. **Offering free feng shui consultations as a service.** I offered one free feng shui consultation per month to any nonprofit, a church or school, for example, as a way to do some good and get my name out there. In exchange, I wrote a blog entry about the organization and the changes they experienced. This worked fine when I ap-

proached my network of church leaders and local teachers directly, but I didn't attract a lot of interest through my website. No one was searching online for this service because it either wasn't wanted or needed, so I stopped. I still wanted to give back to the community, so I do this now by offering a one- to two-hour consult as an auction item for schools and other organizations doing fundraisers. I get about five requests per year. It's still a complimentary consult because the organization receives the gift certificate and whatever auction amount it brings in, and I get to connect with a new client. I'm often offered a free ticket to the event which opens up even more connections. This has been a win/win situation for all.

4. **Working with everyone who called or emailed me.** In the beginning I felt that I had to work with anyone who wanted to work with me. Sometimes I went outside my market area, with travel time taking longer than the appointment! Once I met with someone who wanted to pay me a set fee for unlimited hours of work. I had to learn to say no to services that I don't provide, like purchasing furniture. Until I was clear about "my perfect clients," I was serving everyone. Figure out your niche, what you're good at, and sell that incredibly valuable service to the people who will love you for it and tell the world.

5. **Not taking into account service fees and added time when billing my long-distance clients.** I love doing virtual appointments via video chat apps and have done many over the years. An early mistake was charging the same amount for my services whether they were online or in person. I found that I need time to get to know what the client wants before we "meet" online. This includes reviewing photos and/or floor plans before we talk. I also forgot that when you provide your services online you often incur an online payment service fee. I now include the service fee as part of my hourly rate for the service and add at least thirty minutes of prep time prior to a virtual consultation.

6. **Forgetting to ask for testimonials.** In the beginning I was shy about asking for testimonials and didn't know when to ask for them. Today, I follow up with my clients after their appointment with a specific question, comment, or link regarding their consultation and ask them to write a testimonial. I explain that they can respond to the email or use the links I provide to do a Google or Facebook review. Not everyone does this and that's OK. Some of my clients send a thank you note, text or email, and I use these, too, as testimonials. I also write online testimonials to organizations and businesses that do an outstanding job for me as a customer. If I want testimonials myself, I need to be willing to write them for others. This creates a positive universal energy exchange!

7. **Not doing a vision board.** I started doing vision boards about five years ago and it has changed my life. Not only does this tool help me daily manifest my dreams, but it's a constant reminder of my goals and what I'm grateful for. This powerful, creative business partner (yep, this "partner" reminds me every day what is important!) is your lighthouse when you're feeling lost. Do a vision board every year!

8. **Worrying.** Here's my definition of worry: focusing on what you don't want to happen. Stop doing this and look up at your vision board—focus on what you *do* want to happen instead.

9. **Not following up and thinking I'm a bother!** One of my secret nightmares is having anyone think I'm spamming them. From that viewpoint, it was easy to talk myself out of sending periodic emails. This is a bad idea. Occasional emails, touch-base emails, value-packed emails, announcements that benefit your clients—are all perfect examples of important emails to send.

10.   **Not asking for help.** I saved the best for last. This gets back to the mythical concept of the solopreneur: that made up, I-did-it-all-myself word that implies everything you've done has sprung magically from your head. This is rubbish! One of my favorite sections of any book I've finished reading is the acknowledgments section where authors thank the many people who helped them get to that last page of a published book. I love thinking about all those people—some who read early drafts, others who edited out the misspelled words, the artist who created the cover, the group that marketed the book, the agent who sold it, the friend who brought over soup when things weren't going well. They are all there in the acknowledgments. It's a beautiful thing to have helpers, but you only actually have them if you ask. So, this is my advice: Ask.

I've certainly made more mistakes, but those are my top ten. Mistakes are wonderful learning opportunities. I hope that by sharing some of mine I can help shorten your learning curve so you can get your business up and running with joy and confidence, sooner rather than later!

CHAPTER 9

Wealth & Prosperity A Flow of Gratitude	**Fame & Reputation** The Golden Rule in Action	**Relationships** Get to Know Your Clients
Health & Family You Are the Chief Health Officer	**The Center** Your Stable Base	**Creativity** Express Yourself and Connect with Others
Knowledge & Self-Cultivation Take Care of Yourself	**Career & Journey** How Do You Get to Where You Want to Go?	**Helpful People & Travel** Meet My Helpers

Helpful People & Travel: Meet My Helpers

I'm excited to introduce you to some of my helpers, both seen and unseen. Whether in real life (IRL), online, or invisible to the eye, each has been present for me. I also want to show you how I've put my helpers to work for me, and what happened as a result.

My Helpers Are Legion! I Just Need to Ask.

We live in a country and culture that supports and applauds individual action. We all can name the entrepreneurial, scientific, and creative heroes and heroines of our time. Just refer to their last names and everyone knows who we're talking about, right? Gates. Curie. Winfrey. But the fact is, each of those people became successful because of an abundance of help from others. We can also achieve success—however we define it—if we ask for and receive an abundance of help along the way.

138

I am a huge believer in getting help in whatever form it comes in. I just need to remember to ask. Is this hard for you? You are not alone.

At the root of feng shui is a belief in the inner connectedness of the seen and unseen worlds. As practitioners, we help people change their seen world (their spaces) to impact their unseen world (their thoughts and feelings that lead to action). This same concept relates to asking for help. Feng shui practitioners know that we have both seen and unseen helpers just waiting for us to tap into their generosity.

My seen helpers include anyone who is physically present in my life or their work is available as a book or podcast. Many of them don't live in my town but are there for me via phone, email, or social media. They include family members and friends, teachers, colleagues, contractors, Facebook friends, salesclerks, help staff, authors, podcasters, and my clients! Unseen helpers are the spirits and angels I call upon in prayer and meditation.

Here are some of my real-life heroes and heroines—my seen helpers—for whom I am extremely grateful:

My family, specifically my husband and children. My journey started with my acknowledging that I wanted a different way of being in the world, with a different type of work and job. This was going to change how we lived, and I hoped they'd be on board. They were and are! Thank you, Jim, Milo, and Max.

My feng shui certification school, teachers, colleagues, and retreat attendees. Thank you, Western School of Feng Shui (WSFS): Terah, Amy, Karen, Becky, Liv, and all my feng shui colleagues and retreat attendees: Ro, Gail, Lisa, Jeni, Leah, Laura, Amber, Marsha, Joy, Katrina, Waller, Heather, and Jonni.

My Feng Shui Practitioner Facebook pages. You will find all sorts of Facebook pages for people around the world who have the same interests as you do. Thank you to all my feng shui sisters and brothers out in the ether who share their insights and stories here.

My entrepreneurial gurus. This group has stayed supportive from the moment I asked them if my idea could really become a business. Thank you, Nancy, Wendell, Louisa, Leslie, and Milo.

My first graphic designer. She took my ideas about who I was and what I wanted to do and created an image that became my logo and my brand. Thank you, Kathy.

My web designers, developers, and administrators. Thank you, Eric, Liz, Blizzard Press, Todd, and Linda.

The Denver Public Library (DPL) program directors. Thank you, Kristin, for getting me started, and thank you to all the DPL program directors who have invited me to share feng shui with their patrons.

My videographer and online course helpers. Thank you, Caleb, Felicity, Abe, and Jane. Thank you, Stephen, Kristin, Cynthia, and Andi.

My computer and phone applications. The free or low-cost help available online, right in front of me, is truly mind boggling, and I am profoundly grateful for:

- Canva
- Dropbox
- E-junkie
- Facebook
- FaceTime

- Google Analytics and Google Meet
- LinkedIn
- Mailchimp
- PayPal
- Pinterest
- Skype
- Survey Monkey
- Venmo
- What's App
- WordPress
- Zoom

My business networking groups: The Lowry Business Alliance and the International Feng Shui Guild.

All the podcasters who I've listened to while out walking. Thank you, Shankar Vedantam of *Hidden Brain*, Krista Tippett of *On Being*, Pat Flynn of *Smart Passive Income*, and Dan Harris of *10% Happier*.

Authors of these books: *Big Magic*, by Elizabeth Gilbert; *Essentialism*, by Greg McKeown; *The 4-hour Work Week*, by Tim Ferriss; *Attracting Perfect Customers*, by Stacey Hall & Jan Brogniez; *The Answer*, by John Assaraf and Murray Smith; *Finish*, by Jon Acuff, *The Big Leap*, by Gay Hendricks; *Heal Your Body*, by Louise Hay.

My manifested perfect clients I call up in my daily visualization practice. They are only here at the end of this list because I wouldn't have them at all if it weren't for the help I received from the above helpers. I am so grateful for and learn so much from all my wonderful, inquisitive, open-hearted, open-minded, generous, empathetic, friendly, responsible, kind, positive, hopeful, and inspired clients!

Now, how about those unseen helpers? I've got those in spades, too! To call upon them I use a different approach. Sometimes it's plugging in my headphones, picking up a book, or going online to a take a support course. Sometimes it's stopping each day to sit and be with my thoughts or throwing the *I Ching* coins. Sometimes it's standing in front of my vision board and soaking up the images.

My unseen helpers[11]. These helpers have individual, unique talents. Some of them help me find lost things, others help me with directions, some step out in front of me and sweep my path of obstacles, others sit quietly with me in meditation and prayer. They come with me to every feng shui appointment to help me meet my client's needs. Sometimes I send them out to help others. The more I've called upon this group for help, the more it has grown in size and strength. They are my spiritual LinkedIn that recruits more help when I need it and reminds me to reach out to my seen helpers too. I encourage you to activate your own group by imagining them and asking them for help.

The Sage from the *I Ching*. I use the *I Ching* as a spiritual textbook for going deeper within my own mind to understand the world, drawing upon the help of the Sage, who speaks through its pages. You may have another spiritual book you look to for wisdom and insight, and I hope you do.

My vision board. I created my vision board to activate unseen energy. Connecting with my vision board every day has changed me, my business, my family, my way of being. It is a powerful seen and unseen helper. The images in my vision board (seen) speak directly to my unconscious (unseen) and keep me on track.

---

[11] Many call unseen helpers "angels," and that's a great word to use. Because this word may have different religious connotations for readers, I've used a non-religious word. Plus, it works nicely as an opposite to "seen" helpers. Use whatever word you'd like for this type of amazing helper!

The creative life force. I'm grateful for the help I get from universal creative energy—in feng shui, we call this chi energy—that flows through all things. When we tap into this "flow," we are open to another dimension of thought. I am thankful for this unseen stream of creativity and the ideas that flow from it. The key to asking it for help is to practice. So, I meditate; I play; I pray. I use waiting times, traffic stops, and other breaks in activity as extra time to just be. Help is all around us; simply acknowledging this will bring it closer. Practice, read, meditate, reach for it.

It's there. Ask.

Exercise: List your helpers.

Make a list of all your seen helpers and the ones you need to recruit to help you with your business.

Make a list of your favorite business books and podcasts and think of the authors and speakers as part of your unseen helper team.

Sit quietly and gather your helper-angels. Think of all the ways they could help you, and make some requests.

Help Is on the Way (an Example of Asking for Help)

Recently I hired someone to help me with administrative/website maintenance/email marketing tasks. She's fabulous. How did I find this amazing helper? Did I go crazy on social media, posting an ad on LinkedIn, or create a what's-on-your-mind Facebook post with a photo of me pulling my hair out? Nope. Here's how I found my new helper. Let's call her Linda (because that's her name).

First, I called a friend and feng shui colleague who I know has an administrative helper and asked her what her admin did, how many hours she worked, and what her pay scale was. This was a way for me to get some context and pricing for a situation that was very much like mine. You can do the same kind of inquiry on the internet, but if you're lucky, you have a friend you can call.

After advising me to make a list of tasks I needed help with and to calculate how much I was willing to pay, she reminded me to use my feng shui practice around this activity. I needed to boost the Helpful People & Travel area of my office. I should have thought of this! The situation reminded me of the proverbial cobbler's children not getting their shoes resoled. As a feng shui practitioner I go right to work applying feng shui principles to the areas of my clients' homes and offices I so clearly see need enhancing, but sometimes I forget to apply those same principles to problems of my own I want to solve. I took her advice immediately and made a list of everything I needed help with. I wrote a note about my new amazing helper who could do it all and placed it in the silver box I keep in the Helpful People & Travel area of my desk (lower right-hand corner). I also placed an empty (ready to be filled), pink (the color that mixes thinking and feeling, talking and action), metal (the Metal Element enhances this Bagua area) vase in this area of my office.

Here is the list of tasks I wanted help with:

- Email marketing campaign "tagging and scheduling" through Mailchimp
- Social media marketing scheduling
- General administrative work
- Google Analytics quarterly check-ins
- Updating my WordPress website, checking for broken links, etc.

Here is what my note said:

Dear Helper of Transformation: Bring me the perfect helper, in the form you select, to help me build my business. I will try to get out of the way and allow your guidance to help me explore this idea without rushing in. Thank you xoxo.

With the universe primed and my helpers already working on my behalf, I relaxed a bit and got back to work. That is a crucial step in asking for help: allowing your request to be filled without getting in the way. This is often called faith.

The following week I attended a workshop called "Using Events to Market Your Business." I was interested to learn whether there was something I could do to invite/encourage more attendees to hire me after hosting my own events. Alas, the workshop leader didn't address that topic, but he did talk about not doing the things in your business that you aren't good at and getting back to doing what you are good at as a value proposition for your clients. This is exactly what I was trying to do by hiring some help! It felt good to have corroboration. I felt the little nudge from my unseen helpers, as if they were whispering, Lorrie, you're on the right track (but potentially in the wrong workshop).

Although I didn't get what I thought I was going to get from this workshop, I felt like I had come to the right place at the right time. (My unseen helpers often help me this way!) I ended up meeting Elaine, a podcast entrepreneur, who needed a ride home which I could provide. In the car, I shared that I was looking for some administrative help with the specific tasks I'd outlined. I know you are going guess the rest: she knew someone who fit the bill.

Thank you, universal helpers working on my behalf!

She sent me the contact information an hour later and I acted upon it immediately. I also think this is important: one does have to let the universe know that one is serious and grateful for the help by taking action. I contacted Linda and sent my task list with a query: Do you do this? She got right back with an emphatic YES, and we met a week later. After she reviewed my Google analytics, gave me some valuable advice, and confirmed that she could do all I needed her to do, I could tell we were going to be a match. Then she told me she was an energy healer. Be still my heart! A comrade in healing energy arms! We do similar work: she works with the body and I work with environments. I hired her on the spot.

It took twenty-one days from my initial request to find my perfect administrative support person. There are lots of reasons why I love feng shui, but my favorite is this: It works.

Exercise: What do you need help with right now?

Write a note to your universal helpers with your request. Place it in a silver box or bowl or envelope and place it in the Helpful People & Travel area of your desk (lower right-hand corner), your office, or any room in your house/office (from the front door of your space, the Helpful People & Travel area is in the lower right area). Each time you see it, it will acknowledge your intention.

Patiently wait, listen, and act when you're called to.

The End is Also the Beginning

Writing this book has always been about sharing my experiences so that you can use them to create your own heart-centered business. It has also been an exercise in my personal feng shui practice: setting a goal and creating an environment that supports it. That physical environment includes my vision board—with two images that express my desire to write this book (a book cover graphic and a typewriter with a heart-shaped sheet rolled into it), a whiteboard divided into a Bagua grid filled with sticky notes about a chapter or section topic, my inspiration cards and affirmations.

That environmental support inspired action: daily communing with my vision board, reading and reflecting on my affirmations, reviewing my whiteboard where I'd attached my book outline on those sticky notes (all I had to do was grab one that inspired me and sit down to write). And then I wrote—every day. I am reminded daily how much feng shui has changed my life and made it easier.

What's left to tell you?

I want to talk about confidence. In yourself, in the work you're doing, in the business you're creating, in asking for help, in billing your clients and accepting their money, and in using those funds to create something special in your own life and the world.

As I mentioned in my timeline, I have been privileged to be part of two retreats with fellow feng shui practitioners and heart-centered business-women. Being together, sharing our stories, and learning from one another changed us over the course of these retreats. The best photos taken are at the end, when we all look simply radiant and transformed. This is what confidence does to us all. It imbues us with an inner and outer glow.

Giving and receiving knowledge builds confidence.

Confidence comes from learning something new and using it. Confidence is nurtured when we are seen, heard, and taken seriously. We heart-centered businesspeople sometimes have to defend our desire to do the kind of work we do because it may not be profit motivated or scalable. Confidence comes from trusting yourself that your work is valuable and makes a difference in people's lives. You must believe this. You can nurture this confidence by continuing to read and learn about your craft, by bringing your knowledge and service to your clients, by talking to other business owners about their work, and by practicing your work in your own life. Invest in yourself and you will take yourself seriously.

I'm more confident now in my work after practicing and sharing feng shui since 2009, but I'm still learning new things. Every. Single. Day. I try to come to every client appointment with the eyes of a new practitioner because every space is new to me. There is wonder and joy in stepping over a new threshold. It makes my heart sing every time. Each appointment takes me back to my first. I have more experience now after years of practice as a feng shui consultant, but I feel newly minted at every appointment.

Confidence allows me to let go of trying so hard. Confidence lets me be new and open and alive at each appointment. Confidence helps me to be kind while making recommendations.

Confidence allows me to ask for my fee, accept it with gratitude, and deposit it knowing I'm creating something beneficial with these funds. In feng shui, accruing money is not what wealth and prosperity are all about. Creating abundance is about drawing money to us, being grateful, and then sending it back into the world to create abundance in someone else's world, and on and on in a cycle. I bless all the money that leaves my account—to pay my webmaster, my videographer, my admin support person, my printer, and my service fees, and to cover the costs of products I need to run my business, including donations.

Confidence allows me to ask for help. It takes confidence to acknowledge that we don't know it all. And it takes confidence to show others that we don't know it all. What a gift we give to someone when we ask for and then receive their help. This is yin and yang in practice and in motion. Sometimes we are yang in our asking, and then we must sit in yin, receiving.

Confidence is having the courage to know you're ready to do your work while understanding that you can't know everything, but you go out and do the work anyway. Don't let not having years of experience be a reason not to practice your craft professionally. If you have done the work to be certified in your field, it's time for you to share your gift!

Confidence is forgiving yourself when you make a mistake and asking forgiveness of others when your mistake impacts them. Confidence is forgiving others when their mistakes impact you.

Confidence is hard. It means being an adult about who you are and what you have to give to this world. I'll be honest: I have times when I don't feel like I'm enough. And then I do the work to see myself anew. I look to my vision board, I read my affirmations and my testimonials. I meditate. I work. I rest. I play.

This is the end of my book, but I hope a beginning for you. I hope I have given you some tips on how to create a bedrock of support for your business that will allow you to stand tall in your work and to take it wherever it leads you. The world needs more heart-centered businesses.

The world needs you.

Chapter Notes

Chapter 1. The Center: Your Stable Base

Email Template Example

Example of an email response for a residential feng shui appointment using my templated text highlighted in *italics*.

From: Lorrie Grillo <lwgrillo@thrivingspaces.com>
Date: Thursday, November 14, 2019 at 2:03 PM
To:
Subject: Thank you for asking about Thriving Spaces Feng Shui

Hello Melissa – thanks so much for filling in the questionnaire and giving me some background on your interest in feng shui. I love Denver's older homes; they are treasures. I also find them kind of refreshing now that the style for almost all new buildings is contemporary.

Creating peace, calm and positive energy is what I love to bring to a feng shui consultation. It is what we want to come home to at the end of the day. Our homes are our personal paradises—that place where we can truly be ourselves and relax into the safety and comfort of our shelter. I'd love to help you facilitate this energy, this feeling in your home, for you and your family, and guests.

Here's how I work with my residential clients:

I typically spend about two hours in your home with you. During that time, I'll ask if I can take photos while we tour your home. I'll make recommendations in each room as we walk around. We'll talk about your favorite and least favorite areas, which you've already described to me in your questionnaire. I'll look at your yin/yang balance, discuss the Bagua on the overall plan of the home as well as the individual rooms and make recommendations using the feng shui elements. I can write up all of my recommendations and present them to you in a Priority Report, which I send digitally within a week of our consultation. Your report includes your home's floor plan with the feng shui Bagua drawn on it so you can identify the life areas we discussed during the consultation. The report also includes links to support our discussion – including ideas for furniture, artwork, fixtures, paint colors and furniture placement/layout – to help you understand the feng shui concepts. I use the floor plan with Bagua to prioritize your feng shui recommendations so you can easily remember and create an action plan. I follow up with you to find out how you're doing and answer any questions you may have. You may also take your own notes during the consultation, if you prefer. See options below.

Feng shui In-home Residential Consultation with Priority Report and Bagua layout
    Price

Feng shui In-home Residential Consultation without report (you take notes)
    Price

For either service, you will have a (usually long!) list of ideas that you can implement to help you reach your goals. I'd love to work together, and I have openings next week, if you want to get started.

Thanks again for writing. I hope to hear back from you,

Lorrie

Lorrie Webb Grillo
Certified Practitioner of Essential Feng Shui®
Thriving Spaces Feng Shui

Canva Design Examples

Canva makes it easy to create different size graphics through their many templates. Below are some email headers I made for promoting my vision board workshops. I select a different image and quote every year (these images are from Unsplash, a high-resolution photo website which allows for free usage under their license) as the theme of the workshop. I think this makes the workshop unique and fun for the attendees who return year after year. The email header template in Canva is sized correctly for inserting into an email marketing program; for me, that's MailChimp.

This is an email header that I use as an e-thank you note to those who attend my workshops. You can see that it is branded with the image from my website, business cards, and other marketing materials. With MailChimp, you can personalize the email with your contact's first name.

This is a Facebook "cover" (which is the name of a Canva template sized for the platform) for my Facebook "Home" page. Canva has options for Instagram Posts, YouTube thumbnails, and other social media uploads as well as print and video media templates.

Chapter 3. Knowledge & Self-Cultivation: Take Care of Yourself

Strategic attraction plan for attracting my perfect customers

There are four parts to this plan: a description of my perfect customer, a list of what we have in common, a list of what they can expect from me, and an action plan to continue to attract them! I created this from doing the exercises in *Attracting Perfect Customers* by Stacey Hall and Jan Brogniez, and I review and update it every year.

A description of my perfect customers:

After their query, they are decisive—they make an appointment—either onsite or via Skype—and keep it.

They are on time with their appointment.

They are open to my ideas and willing to try them.

They have what they need to make the changes I recommend: funds, physical and emotional support, and time.

They pay me happily because they value my service and they pay the entire amount at the time of the appointment.

They experience success because they make the changes I recommend. They realize the changes happening to them after the appointment are from their feng shui adjustments.

They refer my services, tell their friends and family about me, and become repeat customers.

They ask great questions that create more opportunities for them and for me to share feng shui.

They hire me again for their office, company, or for their home.

They pay for and attend my workshops, live and online.

They want me to be successful with my business.

They write positive testimonials for me to use on my website and in my social media.

They open my emails and engage with me through live interactions and social media.

They are located within my Denver boundaries and are willing to pay an additional fee if outside the city limits (up to 30 miles). Skype or FaceTime beyond that limit.

They consider me their "feng shui consultant."

They are everywhere!

A list of what my perfect customers and I have in common:

Knowing and believing that change is possible through learning something new and applying it to your life. We create our lives through our visions, thoughts, and actions.

Why do they get up in the morning? Because

- they have a passion and purpose for their lives
- they are seekers

- they believe that their thoughts and actions make a difference
- they are grateful for another day

Who is/are the most important person/s in their world?

- their family
- their friends
- their clients

What is most important to them?

- kindness in their family, their work and in the world
- creating value with their lives – either raising their families and/or through their work
- seeking a higher path – harmony and balance over strife and "being right"
- creating their own happiness and "luck"
- achieving their goals with integrity

What do they want to achieve before they leave this world?

- raising good people (if they have children)
- being responsible for their thoughts and actions
- teaching others by example
- providing valuable service through their work and receiving abundant compensation for it
- kindness to others and their selves

What do they really love about their lives?

- having an opportunity to be here, now, and to make a difference
- their families
- our beautiful planet
- giving and receiving positivity and hope
- creating peace and prosperity for anyone who seeks it

My perfect customers' expectations: *I choose for my perfect customers to expect me to:*

Be on time for our appointment.

Provide the professional services I have spelled out for them in my response to their query email or phone conversation regarding their specific request.

Arrive with an open mind and heart to absorb the energy of their spaces and help them with the exact feng shui adjustments that will help them achieve their goals.

Listen to their needs and respond with feng shui recommendations that meet these needs and create new ways of thinking about their spaces.

Teach them about feng shui so they can continue to use this amazing ancient system to help them after the consultation.

Send their digital report (should they request one) within one week of the appointment.

Provide exceptional value for my fee.

Have a successful business.

Check in with them after the appointment with a specific email about how they are achieving their goals.

Communicate periodically about feng shui workshops and additional services they may choose via email marketing or social media posts.

Have amazing workshops throughout the year that they can attend to boost their knowledge and share feng shui with other like-minded people.

Appreciate them for being a client!

Take care of myself mentally, emotionally, and physically, and continue my education to be the best feng shui consultant I can be.

Have an excellent website, up-to-date blog, and changing Facebook and Pinterest pages.

Donate my services in the form of a gift certificate as a "give back" to the community.

Review my Strategic Attraction Plan every day for 5 minutes!

What do I have to improve to attract more perfect customers?

Review and rejoice with my vision board every day!

Review my Strategic Attraction Plan **every day** for 5 minutes!

Provide excellent live and online workshops throughout the year for them to attend. Vision Board in January, Denver Public Library workshops and other associations, private events, and business opportunities.

Engage with them: write a blog once per month. (Set calendar). Post it on Facebook and LinkedIn. Make sure to link to other pages on my website.

Engage with them: Post on Facebook, Pinterest, OR LinkedIn once per month.

Stay in touch with my clients. Put a tickler in my calendar for a 1-, 3- and 12-month check-in email.

Have faith in this process by working my plan and not worrying.

Participate in my live and online networking groups.

Ask for reviews on Google and Facebook. Post new testimonials on my website.

Speak when invited to!

Read my affirmations!

FOCUS ON THE VITAL FEW ACTIVITIES, NOT THE TRIVIAL MANY.

(Be an Essentialist!)

Chapter 3. Knowledge & Self-Cultivation: Take Care of Yourself.

My favorite feng shui books:

I reread and use these books, as references and inspiration. They are listed alphabetically.

Feng Shui Symbols by Christine M. Bradler and Joachim Alfred P. Scheiner

Feng Shui Your Work Spaces by Sharon Stasney

A Guide to the I Ching by Carol K. Anthony (Third Edition Revised and Enlarged)

I Ching, The Oracle of the Cosmic Way by Carol K. Anthony and Hanna Moog

Move Your Stuff, Change Your Life by Karen Rauch Carter

Sacred Space: Clearing and Enhancing the Energy of Your Home by Denise Linn

The Western Guide to Feng Shui by Terah Kathryn Collins (I enjoy all of Terah's books but this is my bible!)

Chapter 6. Fame & Reputation: The Golden Rule in Action.

My handout or email gift after a talk or workshop: Top 10 things to do when you get home (to boost the energy of your space).

You are practicing feng shui when you create an environment that supports you. Here are my top ten feng shui actions that will immediately boost the energy of your space!

Top 10 things to do when you get home (to boost the energy of your space!)

1) <u>Fix all broken things.</u> Our homes reflect who we are and offer us a metaphor for our lives. Feeling at peace at home starts with feeling safe, so changing light bulbs, fixing broken locks and latches on doors and windows, and leaving an open pathway to your door so you don't trip are all great ways to practice feng shui and help you sigh with relief when you walk in the door.

2) <u>Sleep well and then make your bed every day!</u> If you can, use a headboard, and place the head of the bed against a solid wall so that you can easily see the door and/or windows in the room. This creates a safe and secure place for you to completely relax, let go, and sleep. Then, when you wake, make your bed! This one act of organization

can make a world of difference when you walk into your bedroom at the end of the day.

3) <u>Make space for what you want.</u> Whatever it is that you want more of, clothing, books, relationships, money—make room for it by clearing out/giving away something—clothing, books, relationships, money. Whatever it is, getting rid of what you no longer need opens up opportunity for what you want to come on in.

4) <u>De-clutter and organize what you do have.</u> In feng shui we say Clutter = Stuck Energy. It can be a fun exercise to ask yourself where you feel stuck and then look for clutter around you. Start anywhere—a closet, bookshelf, even a bulletin board.

5) <u>Review your artwork (and hang it at eye level).</u> I had a business client once who couldn't close his deals. On the wall behind him he had a huge canvas of a battle being fought on horseback with guns and swords. Injured men on both sides were in the forefront of the scene. I asked him who was winning this fight and he said he couldn't tell. He said, "It looks like a struggle." And, then he looked at me and smiled and said, "I think I'll take it down." His business picked up the very next day! If you are looking at art that says "struggle" to you, or anything that you don't want in your life, you may choose to take it down. If you want a peaceful paradise to come home to, make sure that your artwork supports that goal. And hang it so you don't have to crank your neck up (or down) to see it.

6) <u>Review your room usage and make adjustments if necessary.</u> This is your home; you make the rules. If doing art at the end of the day relaxes and replenishes you and you don't have a studio—make one. It could be time to get rid of the dining table and create an art studio (or whatever you want!)

7) <u>Keep healthy things around you and get rid of all dead things.</u> There aren't many hard-and-fast rules in feng shui, but this is one of them. Dried flowers invariably are dusty and usually not very attractive. If you want to save a flower arrangement, press the flowers when they are fresh and create art. Rotting food and dead or sick plants should also be thrown away. Happy, healthy plants are wonderful—and if don't have a green thumb, artificial plants are fine—just keep 'em clean.

8) <u>Make sure all doors and windows can be opened fully, without limitation.</u> A door or window that opens freely, as far as it can go, represents your willingness to recognize and embrace new opportunities. So, no storing boxes behind doors that don't get used often and, if possible, no painting windows closed. Doors and windows that open freely offer us fresh air and help to clear out old, musty air (and thoughts).

9) <u>Make sure you can see your entire face or body in your wall or full-length mirror.</u> It was trendy for a while to have small mirrors attached like tiles, to make a larger mirror—only whenever you looked into one of those your face was broken up into pieces! None of us want to feel "broken up" when we look in a mirror, especially at home. This is the same for mirrors that are too small where you can only see part of your face in them. We sometimes call mirrors the "aspirin of feng shui." They reflect light and energy, which can uplift a space. They also express the Water Element, which supports flow and wealth. So, add mirrors to your space and see yourself in your home!

10) <u>Love your space; you are in relationship with it!</u> Make your space your own personal paradise, no matter how temporary it might be. Surround yourself with the items that tell the story of who you are and want to become. When you make your home safe, comfortable, and beautiful for yourself, you are practicing masterful feng shui.

About the Author

Lorrie Webb Grillo is a Certified Practitioner of Essential Feng Shui® and owner of Thriving Spaces Feng Shui, a consulting practice established in 2009. She works with residential and commercial clients, teaches live and online workshops, and writes about feng shui. She is grateful to her wonderful clients who have implemented her feng shui recommendations and reaped the benefits in their lives and businesses, from finding love and starting a family, to changing jobs, welcoming clients and customers, blessing their spaces, and manifesting their visions. She loves the unique nature of every feng shui question and honors all projects, big and small. There are many books about how to practice feng shui but few about how to create a feng shui practice. So, she wrote one.

Connect with Lorrie on her website, www.thrivingspaces.com, take her client questionnaire at https://www.thrivingspaces.com/get-started/, or email her directly at lwgrillo@thrivingspaces.com. You can also find her at https://www.facebook.com/thrivingspaces, https://www.pinterest.com/lwgrillo/_saved/, and https://www.linkedin.com/in/lorriegrillo/.

To receive information about Lorrie's workshops and other news, sign-up here: https://thrivingspaces.us17.list-manage.com/subscribe?u=c068c66011d88f4d7514ec1d6&id=d5147f1bb8.

Made in United States
North Haven, CT
13 May 2022

19117973R00107